IN THE NATIONAL INTEREST:

THE 1990 URBAN SUMMIT

IN THE NATIONAL INTEREST:

THE 1990 URBAN SUMMIT

With Related Analyses, Transcript, and Papers

Volume Editors:

Ronald Berkman, *The City University of New York*
Joyce F. Brown, *The City University of New York*
Beverly Goldberg, *The Twentieth Century Fund*
Tod Mijanovich, *The Twentieth Century Fund*

The Twentieth Century Fund Press/New York/1992

Library of Congress Cataloging-in-Publication Data

In the national interest : the 1990 Urban Summit with related analyses, transcripts, and papers/volume editors: Ronald Berkman. . . [et al.].

   p. cm.

   1. Urban policy—United States—Congresses.   2. Cities and towns—United States—Congresses.   I. Berkman, Ronald.
HT 123.U765   1990
307.76'0973—dc20   91-39052
ISBN 0-87078-332-7 : $10.95   CIP

Published by The Twentieth Century Fund Press
41 East 70th Street, New York, New York 10021

Foreword

Our nation's largest cities, scattered across a vast geographical area, marked by different economic bases, climates, racial mixtures, face the same array of seemingly unsolvable problems—poverty, drugs, declining infrastructures, racism, eroding economic bases, school systems in chaos, and middle-class flight. The big-city mayors who run these huge urban centers belong to major organizations that represent all those that govern municipalities, but their problems are different both in scale and intensity from those facing most of their colleagues.

In the fall of 1990, reacting to the fading federal interest in America's urban problems, New York City's Mayor David N. Dinkins invited the mayors who represented the largest of our nation's cities, those with populations of about a quarter of a million or more, to come together to discuss their unique problems. Thirty-five mayors and their representatives seized that opportunity to discuss the special problems they face and to try to find a way to raise the consciousness of all Americans to the value of these large cities, which together house some 80 percent of corporate America.

The group was determined from the outset to present a picture of the value of cities as well as their problems. They were determined to formulate a detailed and specific agenda for national action. And they succeeded. They achieved a surprising degree of consensus about both the nature of the difficulties they confront and the possible solutions to them, which are presented in the Urban Compact that is included in this volume.

The mayors were assisted in their efforts by a group of experts on urban problems, some of whose papers are included in this volume. The paper writers are also the nucleus of a developing urban research network that has been formed to provide mayors of large urban areas with information and ideas for dealing with the difficult problems facing their cities.

The Twentieth Century Fund, a nonpartisan public policy research organization that has long been interested in urban affairs, is happy to contribute to the efforts of the mayors through support for the editing and publishing of this report. Our contribution is part of our annual contribution to the city of New York in lieu of taxes in return for municipal services provided by the city. As part of its regular program, the Fund recently supported a Task Force on Housing whose report, *More Housing, More Fairly*, made specific recommendations aimed at making housing more affordable for all citizens. It is also supporting major works investigating the relative value of various types of programs for the homeless, the relationship between poverty and drugs, new ways to fight racism and poverty, and how efforts to help the poor have succeeded and failed.

I would like to thank two Fund staff members, Beverly Goldberg and Tod Mijanovich, for their volunteer efforts on this publication project. I would like as well to take this opportunity to recognize the contributions of Ronald Berkman and Joyce F. Brown of the City University of New York.

Richard C. Leone, President
The Twentieth Century Fund
December 1991

TABLE OF **C**ONTENTS

PREFACE

As Mayor of the City of New York, and as an individual who is deeply concerned about the direction of federal policy in this country, I believe that the book that you are about to read is of critical importance. It is a discussion of our future—and the steps we must take to rebuild our cities, and our entire nation, in the coming decades.

This book chronicles an important partnership that was launched in November 1990 in New York City—an Urban Summit of mayors from thirty-five leading U.S. cities, intended to reestablish the prominence of urban America in our nation's political discourse and develop a comprehensive agenda for the social, economic, and cultural future of all America.

We gathered as leaders of the urban communities that are the very core of American life—and we banded together to reassert our crucial role in this country's economic and cultural life, and to demand the attention and the resources that are long overdue.

The importance of cities to this country is well documented. Our cities are the centers of commerce—leading our nation in trade, manufacturing, finance, law, and communications. Cities have been our historic and cultural capitals, paving the way to freedom and democracy throughout the world.

Our cities serve as the gateways to America for millions of richly diverse immigrants, keeping the American dream of participation and opportunity alive as we enter the 1990s; and our cities serve as America's gateways to the rest of the world—bringing our economy and culture to peoples and economies in every part of the world. It is no exaggeration to say that our cities are the engine that pulls America into the future.

In the past ten years, however, we have witnessed the painful withdrawal of our federal government from urban life—at a time when our needs are greater than ever. In 1990, federal funds comprised 19.4 percent of New York City's budget. At the end of a decade of shameless neglect of urban America, that share has shriveled to 9.7 percent in 1990—and each of my colleagues in cities across American can tell a similar tale.

Federally subsidized housing programs have been slashed by 82 percent in the Reagan-Bush years. Our urban poor have been especially hard hit. Ten years ago, the word "homeless" wasn't even in our dictionary. Now the word defines a human tragedy of such a profound scale that it is difficult to describe in words. Nearly 20 percent of our children are now living in poverty—the worst record in the industrialized West. The gap between rich and poor hasn't been this great since America's Gilded Age. The income share of our poorest citizens has fallen to $3,504 a year while the income of the wealthiest has doubled to $404,566 a year.

As the crippling inequities of the past decade unfold, local leaders—those who deliver services directly, and who are most accountable to the people—must seize the initiative for honest and progressive change. We are prepared to show strong leadership—to assume the responsibility of providing quality education, sound infrastructure, job training, and employment opportunities. But we need greater resources—not fewer—to reach our goals. Without resources, we won't have even a fighting chance.

Fortunately, the people of this country stand behind us. In November 1990, the City University of New York's Office of Urban Affairs released its nationwide survey, "America and Its Cities: A Nation that Cares." That title says it all, for the survey found that a great majority of Americans like and care about their cities, and that those who live in the adjoining suburban communities are willing to help urban centers solve their vexing social and economic problems.

On this issue, it seems that the public is a few steps ahead of our government in Washington; and it is important that our suburban neighbors support us—because we must include them in our new coalition. For all the simplistic talk of Democratic-liberal cities and Republican-conservative suburbs, this alliance is a natural and an essential one; for when our cities prosper, so do our suburbs; and when our cities suffer and decay, suburban dwellers also feel an encroaching sense of insecurity.

The challenges our cities face are the challenges that America faces. They must be met by all Americans, working together. The Urban Summit was not a one-time effort—although I believe that we have accomplished a great deal. Rather, the Urban Summit was the beginning of a new era of urban cooperation.

Together, we must fight to ensure long-term fiscal stability, despite a weakening national economy. Together, we must bring our cities—and our nation—into a position of even greater economic strength, to tap into the exciting changes in our world economy. Together, we must devise creative new approaches to our common problems, and work with one another to find solutions.

I am grateful to have such a talented group of colleagues as mayors of this nation's leading cities. Of course, we have come to our current positions from vastly different backgrounds—and with vastly different political and social agendas. But we share a deep commitment to urban life and urban issues that overrides those differences. I have been honored to work with this distinguished group, and I sincerely hope that our efforts, as described in this book, will provide a solid foundation for the future of our cities and our society.

David N. Dinkins
New York City
November 1991

Editors' Introduction

The Urban Summit Conference held on November 12-14, 1990, was an auspicious occasion. In response to an invitation from New York City's Mayor David N. Dinkins, thirty-five mayors representing the millions of Americans who reside in our nation's largest cities came to Manhattan to discuss the problems they and their cities faced in an era of devolution of federal responsibilities to the states and municipalities and a general economic downturn. The purpose of the meeting was to find a way to present the unique case of the cities to all America—their role as centers of industry, as centers of our nation's cultural and intellectual activities, and as centers of social problems.

The Summit was not to be a one-time event, but the start of an ongoing attempt to solve the special problems of cities and change the way that Americans view them. No one yet knows if the Summit will make a difference in the long-term, but some immediate benefits made the effort more than worthwhile. First, it allowed the mayors, in their closed session, to freely exchange ideas with their peers, gaining an understanding of how universal their problems were and a feeling that they were part of a group that was working in the face of incredible pressures to make a difference. Second, a committee of mayors has continued to pursue the goals outlined in the Urban Compact and has met with the leaders of the U.S. Congress to advance the legislative agenda. Mayors have met with chief executive officers from major U.S. corporations to explore new opportunities for partnerships. A number of cities have sponsored regional summits to strengthen the ties of cities and suburbs within metropolitan areas. Third, it resulted in the establishment of an Urban University Research Network, which will tap into the resources of the incredible array of scholarly institutions based in our cities to provide support and guidance and information to the mayors.

The other result is what you are holding in your hands. This volume is aimed at summing up the work of the Summit. It contains an edited transcript of the more than seven hundred pages of discussions that took place at the Summit; it also contains the Urban Compact issued by the mayors, their position paper; and it contains a collection of papers by some of the foremost scholars and researchers on the issues facing our cities. It is aimed at increasing our understanding of what our cities are, the difficulties they face in terms of public perceptions and media coverage, the social issues they confront, and the efforts that have been and should be made to help them.

RB▴JFB▴BG▴TM

Mayors Attending

MAYOR JERRY ABRAMSON, Louisville, Kentucky

MAYOR HECTOR LUIS ACEVEDO, San Juan, Puerto Rico

MAYOR ART AGNOS, San Francisco, California

MAYOR SIDNEY BARTHELEMY, New Orleans, Louisiana

MAYOR BOB BOLEN, Fort Worth, Texas

MAYOR TOM BRADLEY, Los Angeles, California

MAYOR LEE COOKE, Austin, Texas

MAYOR RICHARD M. DALEY, Chicago, Illinois

MAYOR DAVID N. DINKINS, New York City, New York

MAYOR KANE DITTO, Jackson, Mississippi

MAYOR CLAY DIXON, Dayton, Ohio

MAYOR RAYMOND FLYNN, Boston, Massachusetts

MAYOR DONALD FRASER, Minneapolis, Minnesota

MAYOR SANDRA W. FREEDMAN, Tampa, Florida

MAYOR WILSON GOODE, Philadelphia, Pennsylvania

MAYOR RICHARD GREENE, Arlington, Texas

MAYOR MAYNARD JACKSON, Atlanta, Georgia

MAYOR PAUL HELMKE, Fort Wayne, Indiana

MAYOR WALTER T. KENNEY, Richmond, Virginia

MAYOR BOB KNIGHT, Wichita, Kansas

MAYOR GERALD McCANN, Jersey City, New Jersey

MAYOR JOHN McHUGH, Toledo, Ohio

MAYOR MARY CHAPAR MORAN, Bridgeport, Connecticut

MAYOR P. J. MORGAN, Omaha, Nebraska

MAYOR JOHN NORQUIST, Milwaukee, Wisconsin

MAYOR MAUREEN O'CONNOR, San Diego, California

MAYOR FEDERICO PEÑA, Denver, Colorado

MAYOR NORMAN RICE, Seattle, Washington

MAYOR JOSEPH P. RILEY, JR., Charleston, South Carolina

MAYOR JAMES SCHEIBEL, St. Paul, Minnesota

MAYOR KURT SCHMOKE, Baltimore, Maryland

MAYOR HENRY J. SPALLONE, Yonkers, New York

MAYOR XAVIER SUAREZ, Miami, Florida

MAYOR BETTY TURNER, Corpus Christi, Texas

MAYOR MICHAEL WHITE, Cleveland, Ohio

THE COMPACT

PREAMBLE

Like a mighty engine, urban America pulls all of America into the future. America's cities are critical to our national security and economic competitiveness. It is impossible to consider the nation and its cities separately; their fates have always been joined. This is why America's big-city mayors have come together to discuss the future of America.

Urban centers are the focus of national vitality in trade, manufacturing, finance, law and communications. Cities preserve the lion's share of America's history in their museums, libraries, and architecture, and educate a large proportion of America's future in their schools and universities. American culture is profoundly affected by the artistic and intellectual communities that thrive in the compressed space of cities, spawning advances in every aspect of our lives.

America's social compact has frayed. The mayors meeting today challenge other public officials, business, labor, and intellectual leaders—and indeed all Americans—to join us in forging a renewed sense of common purpose and shared endeavor. This new social compact will, in turn, strengthen our national competitiveness.

International leadership and national security are increasingly defined by excellence in education, public safety, and economic prosperity. Economic performance is a national security issue.

The American economy is, in reality, comprised of regional economies centered in America's cities, within which the fates of central cities, suburbs, and rural areas are entwined.

Therefore, American cities must establish new partnerships in order to generate the support—both in policy and in funding—that is needed if the nation is to retain and enhance its position as an international leader.

NEW URBAN PARTNERSHIPS

Given the changes of the last decade in America's economic and political alignments, we must new our commitment to existing coalitions and forge new partnerships. At the most fundamental level, there must be a coalition among us, the mayors of America's largest cities. This Summit is the first step in a process of revitalizing our coalition and renewing awareness among our constituents.

"

We must work to improve our relationships with business, labor, and our constituents. We must forge more durable connections with cities and suburbs in the metropolitan economy. As mayors, we are eager to work as partners with the president and the Congress, but the relationship between cities and the federal government must be based on an efficient and just distribution of resources and responsibilities.

Americans participate in politics when they see the connection between policy debates and their day-to-day existence. We must take a leadership role in informing our residents about the effects of federal policy on their lives, and encouraging them to register to vote and to participate in the civic life of our cities.

It is vital that cities and suburbs coalesce around economic plans for the entire region, and also around political issues of mutual concern. Metropolitan coalitions will inevitably need to address issues that were formerly the sole province of major urban centers. The creation of these coalitions will lead to greater political leverage in state houses and in Washington, D.C.

GOAL: FORGE NEW PARTNERSHIPS TO SUPPORT METROPOLITAN NEEDS.

OBJECTIVES:

- ▲ Develop measurable national goals for improvements in the cities by the year 2000.
- ▲ Create and support legislative initiatives for the urban agenda, e.g., the Competitive Cities Act of 1991 and the Urban Schools of America Act.
- ▲ Design a public education campaign around the theme of why cities are essential; redefine "city" to include the entire urban region as a community.
- ▲ Identify and develop partnerships with all levels of government as well as with business, education, media, and labor.

ACTION ITEMS:

1. Meet with President Bush and the congressional leadership in 1991 to pursue a national urban agenda.

2. Inject urban issues into 1992 presidential, congressional, and other campaigns, by:
   - ▲ Seek debates among presidential candidates in 1991 with mayors asking the questions, to be held in several different regions of the nation.
   - ▲ Targeting priority urban issues for the 1992 election platforms.
   - ▲ Establishing voter awareness programs within their cities.

- ▲ Involving citizens and community leaders in lobbying efforts for state and federal urban programs.

3. Congressional Partnerships

- ▲ Seek passage of "motor-voter" legislation (i.e., automatic voter registration upon vehicle registration.)
- ▲ Seek creation of a Congressional Urban Caucus.
- ▲ Maintain and publish an annual "urban scorecard" on how members of Congress and the administration support the urban agenda.
- ▲ Support passage of the Brady Bill, which would impose a 7-day waiting period for the purchase of a gun, and support a ban on all domestically manufactured semi-automatic weapons.

4. Metropolitan Regional Partnerships

- ▲ Encourage mayors to call a 1991 meeting with cities and counties in the surrounding region to discuss common issues such as mutual policy objectives, joint economic projects, and elimination of duplicative services.
- ▲ Consider formation of regional partnerships and tax-sharing around specific issues: e.g., solid waste, air pollution, water pollution, transportation.
- ▲ Work with National Association of Counties to organize a meeting between mayors and urban county officials.

5. Business Partnerships

- ▲ Invite corporate leaders to a 1991 national summit to expand city/business partnerships.
- ▲ Explore additional mayoral contacts with national and international corporations through the Business Roundtable, Chamber of Commerce, etc., to secure legislation and financial support for investment in urban America.

6. Mayoral Partnerships

- ▲ Designate the 1990s as the "Decade of the City."
- ▲ Form mayoral "SWAT teams" to conduct issue-oriented forums in several locations throughout America to elevate the national awareness of the urban agenda and the critical importance of cities to national prosperity.
- ▲ Continue to press for a fair and accurate 1990 Census count.

7. University Partnerships

- ▲ Develop a research network among urban universities to study problems and issues common to cities, as well as to make policy recommendations.

CITIES IN THE GLOBAL ECONOMY

Cities are the hubs of the international economy, without which the wheels of commerce will not turn. The new international mobility of business has created a much greater need to connect worldwide operations. Distribution networks are larger and more complex. Capital markets require instantaneous transactions with financial centers across the globe. Specialization of services demands extensive organization and communication systems to bring those services to their users. Only central cities can be the coordinating points in the world's geometrically expanding business networks.

It is time to enlist the support of federal and state government, as well as the national and international corporations who headquarter in America's cities. We must create partnerships that will empower cities with the ability to foster both economic growth and economic justice, and will allow them to prepare and educate a workforce that is sufficiently skilled to compete in the international arena.

Cities have always been centers of commerce and ports of opportunity. The economy of the future can best flourish in cities —where information, education, expertise, and trade all come together.

Today, new frontiers are before us—in trade with Canada, Europe, South America, Africa, and Asia, and in growing industries such as telecommunications, environmental protection, and medical research. We must exert our leadership in these areas to ensure that the residents of our cities—particularly our young people—benefit from these new opportunities.

GOAL: MAINTAIN AND ENHANCE AMERICA'S INTERNATIONAL ECONOMIC LEADERSHIP.

OBJECTIVES:

- ▲ Develop a better-educated and better-prepared workforce.
- ▲ Improve coordination among cities in well-defined regional economic areas.
- ▲ Identify fiscal resources for improvement of key infrastructure elements, including transportation networks, and waste disposal systems.
- ▲ Enact federal and state legislative and other initiatives to enhance the economic competitiveness of cities.

ACTION ITEMS:

1. Call for a Competitive Cities Act of 1991, which would include the following strategies:
   - ▲ incentives for investing in our cities, including: an expanded

"enterprise zone" proposal to ensure local residents' participation in the expanded opportunities the zone will provide; new incentives for investing in research and development, minority- and women-owned projects, and public/private partnerships; a removal of the volume cap on tax-exempt bonds to advance such areas as housing, mass transit, and solid waste infrastructure development.

- ▲ A trade and economic development partnership that would provide funding, part of which would have to be spent in approved "enterprise" or "economic opportunity" zones with a percentage set aside for community-based projects.

- ▲ Federal contract "linkage" requirements that in all federal contracts over a set amount the grantee must establish a program of summer or after-school employment, apprenticeships, or mentoring of disadvantaged youths.

- ▲ A "Computer Corps" to provide instruction to inner-city youths and adults in computer literacy skills. Additional support would be provided for establishing non-profit "computer access centers" in the inner city.

- ▲ A "Work to Learn" program through which high school students from poor to middle income families would have summer and after-school wages matched by a federal set-aside which would pay for a college or vocational education.

2. Take a leadership role in the restructuring of our troubled education system, by:

- ▲ Demanding that the federal Headstart program be an entitlement.

- ▲ Ensuring that children are safe, healthy, and ready to learn when they enter school by demanding increased federal, state, and local support for preschool and early childhood education. Direct funding for such programs is essential.

- ▲ Working for full funding and local implementation of the recently passed child care bill which includes provision of child care services, after-school enrichment programs, and school-based health care for every child who needs such services.

- ▲ Working for tax-exempt programs for business and individual support for local schools and education programs.

- ▲ Demanding further federal and state support for innovative urban school improvements designed to reverse drop-out trends, to support the children of families in crisis, to prepare students for higher education and technological careers, and to train and recruit teachers.

- ▲ Providing municipal government apprenticeships for academically promising high school students, and encourage the development of training programs in the private sector.
- ▲ Sending a delegation of mayors to attend the Urban Education Summit in Washington, D.C., January 13 - 14, 1991, and support the "Urban Schools of America Act" proposed by the Council of Great City Schools.

3. Demand federal reauthorization of legislation to aid our infrastructure, such as the Surface Transportation and Clean Water Acts.

4. Examine further new proposals for urban reinvestment, such as the creation of a national exchange for home and apartment mortgages and retention of a transaction fee for each trade.

FISCAL CHALLENGES

The causes of fiscal strain in city economies are complex. Cities are faced with an extraordinarily difficult mission and must do without the financial, legal, jurisdictional, and political means to create comprehensive solutions—in large measure because of the limits on local governments set by state constitutions and federal appropriations requirements. The federal government does not suffer under such constraints or endeavor to function within the discipline of a balanced budget.

The property tax was designed to pay for basic public services such as fire, water, and police. Revenues from property taxes will never be sufficient to meet the national challenges of educating America's future workforce, winning the war on drugs, caring for persons with AIDS and other health problems, and housing America's homeless population. There must be a clear understanding of the respective roles of federal, state, and municipal governments in finding relief for these national emergencies.

GOAL: DEFINE THE APPROPRIATE ROLES OF THE FEDERAL, STATE, AND LOCAL GOVERMENTS IN ADDRESSING AMERICA'S NEEDS.

OBJECTIVES:

- ▲ Ensure a just return of state and federal taxes generated by city-based businesses and individuals.
- ▲ Ensure that those governmental bodies that establish new programmatic mandates, and take credit at election time for achieving popular goals, take responsibility to provide revenues to cities that must implement these grand objectives.

ACTION ITEMS:

1. Call for the federal government to revise the newly adopted budget process, which now prohibits any shift from defense spending to domestic programs.

2. Demand that federal and state governments fully fund programs to deal with the following national problems:

   ▲ Drug abuse, including adequate funding directly to cities of anti-drug programs to support law enforcement, education, rehabilitation, and treatment on demand.

   ▲ AIDS care and prevention, including full funding of the Ryan White AIDS CARE Act, and Medicaid coverage of HIV-positive patients.

   ▲ Homelessness and Housing, including full funding of the Stewart B. McKinney Homeless Act, the Community Development Block Grant Program, and the newly passed housing bill.

   ▲ Health Care, with particular emphasis on hospitals serving a disproportionate share of indigent patients.

3. Streamline federal categorical grant programs, regulations, and requirements to allow greater flexibility at the local level.

4. Seek passage of state and federal laws that will bar any future unfunded mandates applying to local governments.

5. Call for passage of federal legislation to allow state and local governments to collect sales tax on catalog sales. Without this legislation, there is an inequity between local retailers and nationwide catalog sales outlets.

And the Mayors Said . . .

The following pages contain some of the highlights of the discussions that took place at the Urban Summit. Given limited space, it is impossible to present all the ideas put forth by the mayors—who were intent on carefully explaining what it was about cities that made them so special, and so difficult, and what they proposed be done to ease the problems facing America's cities. Speaking as they did, behind closed doors, the mayors interacted as a group of peers, not only telling one another what they knew, but eager to discover what they could about how others in their unique position felt and believed needed to be done. There were differences of opinion, but more agreement than disagreement—as is evidenced by the Urban Compact presented above, which they all signed. We have tried here, by reordering and editing the 700 pages of transcript, to capture the full flavor and scope of what went on in those sessions.

THE MAYORS BEGAN BY HIGHLIGHTING THE IMPORTANCE OF CITIES TO OUR NATION.

MAYOR BRADLEY:

The importance of mayors and city government, of cities themselves, is not sufficiently appreciated. If America's cities fail in the 1990s, if crime, congestion, pollution, and the lack of family amenities drive a large percentage of city residents out to distant suburbs or small towns, if "not in my backyard" is an acceptable response, and higher costs render cities unable to expand and improve their airports, harbors, waste water treatment plants, landfills, and road networks, if urban schools cannot graduate students prepared to work in the industries where growth will occur, then America's prosperity, quite simply, is in peril.

MAYOR NORQUIST:

We are a priority for the people. Local government services, municipal services, are the most relevant services to people. Cities are the most relevant level of government there is. We have to get the federal government to understand that, along with the media and the business community and everybody else. We have to get them to think that it's in their enlightened self-interest to invest in cities.

MAYOR ABRAMSON:

We're called on to be the financial center and the cultural center and the center for museums and the center of education and the center of government; we're also called on to be the center for homelessness, for the indigent, for health care, etc. So if you redefine the term "city" as community, and community as common interest, you begin to say to suburbanites: you can't be a suburb of nowhere. You must be a suburb of somewhere, and that "somewhere" is the city, the heart of the community.

MAYOR GOODE:

We've not yet been able to define ourselves in a way that sends a clear message to those in Washington and in our state capitals that cities are vital resources, and therefore there are some things that they ought to do to help solve these basic problems. Until we do that, we're going to continue to be perceived as, on the one hand, begging with a tin cup, and on the other, as asking someone to bail us out.

MAYOR MORAN:

The cities are the hub of this country, and without that hub, America will not be able to turn that wheel.

THE MAYORS THEN TURNED TO THE PROBLEMS FACING OUR CITIES

MAYOR RILEY:

We have to keep pointing out that our cities have a disproportionate number of the poor, the needy, the victims of AIDS, the homeless, as well as our colleges, universities, and museums, our culture and our hopes. All of those are in the cities, yet increasingly, the national resources remain outside our cities.

MAYOR RICE:

We face some troubling new realities in education, and our cities have some special needs. For example, our urban school systems enroll a disproportionately large share of the nation's poor and at-risk youth. Over one-third of the nation's poor students attend urban schools. The academic performance of the average inner-city public school system lags below that of most other school systems. The shortage of teachers is two-and-a-half times greater for urban schools. Seventy-five percent of urban school buildings are over twenty-five years old; the facilities are too often in serious disrepair and constitute a poor and demoralizing learning and working environment.

MAYOR NORQUIST:

When the public thinks about what we're asking for as cities, they think we're asking for welfare. That's the image. The mayors meet, they want funding, but cities never really ask for a welfare program. Welfare programs are the federal government's way of not paying attention to problems. The real problem is that the welfare system is such a failure. We should stop trying to reform it; we should scrap it, inaugurate a new approach, one that offers more of what the people want, what we believe in—jobs. We should offer people assurances that if they work full-time we'll supplement their wages so they won't be poor, and we'll help with child care and basic health care.

MAYOR BRADLEY:

Eighty percent of crime in our city is related directly or indirectly to drugs. The whole Southern California area is now the import target for cocaine from Central America, South America, Mexico, and for heroin coming in from the Far East. Unless we control drugs, we can forget it. This is not just about drug abuse, it's about the importation of drugs, it's about the interdiction of drugs, it's about treaties, it's about the chemicals that we send to Colombia that made possible the creation of cocaine in the first place. It is about snuffing out the drug traffic at its source.

THE MAYORS ALSO REFLECTED ON THE COSTS OF THE PROBLEMS THAT THEIR CITIES ARE FACING.

MAYOR DINKINS:

Cities offer hope to those fleeing economic and political persecution. Between 1930 and 1980, America's cities built the greatest economic machine in human history. But since 1980 our creativity in meeting the challenges of urban America has been severely tested, not by any disappearance of will on the part of our people, but by the painful withdrawal of the federal government from American urban life, in housing and child care, in mass transit and public education, in drug enforcement and medical services. The federal government has been on the retreat.

MAYOR RILEY:

Speaking the truth when people aren't listening is never any fun, and maybe it gets old, but I really think that this Summit has to begin by speaking the truth and saying very strongly that our national government has made a huge mistake, a colossal blunder.

In 1980, our country tried to cut taxes and make everybody think things were rosy. At no time in the 1980s did someone come forward and say revenue sharing was a mistake or the community development block grant can't work because it was built on unwise premises, or deny that American cities are where most of the poor and needy people in this great country of ours live. It was simply a policy of appeasement, to get us to close our eyes and ignore the facts. We are paying and will continue to pay the price for that error.

MAYOR BARTHELEMY:

I think we all know our problems, we all know what we need. It seems to me that the problem has been we can't get the White House or our congressional delegations as a whole to understand what our problems are on the local level, and because of that, they have not only taken away money from us, but they have put more responsibility on us. At the same time, they have not given us the means by which we could help ourselves.

THE MAYORS THEN ADDRESSED THE NEED FOR CITIES TO BECOME MORE COMPETITIVE, ESPECIALLY GIVEN THE CURRENT INTERNATIONAL ENVIRONMENT.

MAYOR FRASER:

Most of us have embraced the idea of internationalizing our economies: we supported the opening of trade relationships with other countries around the world, but we've done so uncritically and that's been a mistake. I think the fact that we are now forcing American workers to compete against two-dollar-an-hour jobs in Mexico or Taiwan or Korea has led to the lack of increase in the average wage rate for American workers over the past ten or fifteen years. Moreover, when our industrial jobs have moved overseas, they've been replaced with service jobs that don't pay as much. Thus, we've made the poor poorer, and that has directly affected American cities. If we can demonstrate that that is the outcome of the internationalization of our economy, then it seems that we have a claim on Congress to help redress the balance. Although I've always favored open trade, in theory, if we make our boundaries totally porous, we will become a mirror image of those other societies, and they, at least in the third world, have extraordinary income disparities. We need to think about this in terms of the free trade agreement with Mexico.

MAYOR SPALLONE:

How many jobs do we stand to lose next year if we're not competitive? Make no mistake about it. The global race is big, and it's important because those that are left out will lose. We cannot sustain the infrastructure of our cities, we cannot sustain our social programs without money.

THE MAYORS FOCUSED ON EDUCATION AS ONE OF THE KEYS TO COMPETITIVENESS. AND ONE OF THE KEYS TO ENSURING A BETTER EDUCATIONAL SYSTEM WAS, THEY AGREED, INVOLVING CORPORATIONS IN EDUCATION.

MAYOR RICE:

I think that when we talk about the global economy and how we compete, it comes back to our children and how well they're educated and how well they are integrated into our work force. If we are not educating those children to compete, we cannot be a strong nation, we cannot compete globally.

MAYOR DIXON:

Education is really key to making us competitive in the global market. We need to develop incentives that will not only help local businesses, but will create jobs at the local level that would go to the local youth.

MAYOR BRADLEY:

The local educational systems failed to prepare the work force adequately to fill the jobs available, and so chronic unemployment continues to plague unskilled and semiskilled workers. Sixty percent of our graduates from high school fail to pass the examinations that they take in order to get into the major private corporations of this country.

MAYOR COOKE:

IBM has picked Austin as the urban school district in America that they're going to team up with and work on to ensure that it's a strong district. I think other corporations in America, and international ones that are doing business in America, face much the same problem we do. I think we've got to go and reach out to that community and tell them we want partnerships.

MAYOR SUAREZ:

We need a support system for apprenticeships, for setting up tracks for youngsters to go to schools, and I would even suggest greater priority be given to supporting early childhood development. We should be battling for a universally eligible program for children before they enter school so that they end up on a level playing field. Our taxpayers are saying that we want to see that money is spent where we need it most—in basic education and in nutrition support for children before they enter school.

MAYOR McCANN:

I think early childhood education should be the priority of our education agenda. Put the focus on the disadvantaged children that need help before they reach the school system, so that by the time they come to school, they're not developmentally behind.

THERE WAS A STRONG CONSENSUS THAT THE CITIES MUST FORM NEW PUBLIC/PRIVATE PARTNERSHIPS AND STRENGTHEN THOSE THAT ALREADY EXIST. IN THIS PARTICULAR EXCHANGE, THE MAYORS BEGAN WITH A DISCUSSION OF CORPORATE PARTNERSHIPS AND THEN EXTENDED THE THEME TO PUBLIC/PUBLIC PARTNERSHIPS—PARTNERSHIPS

WITH THE FEDERAL GOVERNMENT AND SUBURBS WITHIN THE METROPOLITAN REGIONS.

MAYOR TURNER:

Our compact must clearly state that there is a consensus here, that the problem lies in our inability to control our own destiny, that we would like opportunities to do a number of things. For example, we'd like the federal government to provide us with some creative tools that would encourage investment. We certainly need to look at partnerships, pub-lic/private partnerships—I don't have the clout to go to Washington and say this is what the cities in Texas need. But we do collectively have the clout.

MAYOR COOKE:

I think we've got to reach out to the business community and tell them we want partnerships. I think we go to the top rungs because I believe they want to help. IBM realizes that there is a fundamental problem in urban school districts in America. I think corporations in America and international companies that are doing business in America are natural partners.

MAYOR WHITE:

I believe we have to search for a partner nationally, and the one partner that we have not talked enough about is the one partner that has a lot at stake if we go down the tubes, big business in America—the IBMs and the Xeroxes and those major national and international corporations that make their homes in our cities. Now, it's one thing for all of us here to get on the Metroliner at night and go to Washington and beg for money for ourselves, but if we are in Washington with the presidents of IBM, Xerox, and other major corporations, and they are saying the same things that we are, that makes it much harder for the federal government to walk away from the message.

MAYOR DALEY:

How do you build coalitions today when you don't have a political organization—Republican or Democrat—and you're not going to have one in the future? You have to go to business leaders to build a coalition for approaching Congress or the executive branch.

The private/public partnership is important because business executives are the ones who are going to influence Congress; they're the ones who are going to influence editorial boards; they're the ones who are going to influence members of the general assembly and state government, our governors.

MAYOR ABRAMSON:

If it's going to work, you've got to generate that "ouch" factor with the private sector to make them realize that it's their fight, too. We did that about five, six years ago in Louisville. A Fortune 500 company couldn't find computer operators. They brought fifty folks in from out of the county, and all of a sudden the business community realized that it was in its best interest to begin to make sure that the children coming out of the public school system were computer literate. When you can grab business people by the bottom line, their hearts and wallets will follow every time. The next thing you know, we raised $10 million and created computer labs in every school—now we have one computer for every eleven children, from kindergarten to senior year. When our children graduate, they can get those jobs. In our case the ouch factor rose to a level where the business sector said it wanted to participate.

MAYOR SPALLONE:

When you talk about cities and business partnerships, I think one of the things that's important if you're looking for success is unions. I think unions have a rightful place in any partnership with business organizations and government. Unions have a great impact, so it's important to bring them in, and then you have all parties involved in urban improvement and development. To leave out union leadership is a mistake.

MAYOR DITTO:

My concern is the implementation of our agenda, however it may turn out. If we do not bring in the private sector, including foundations and corporations for funding, using the clout that these people have, I do not see us getting anything done. I see no one standing behind us to get the kind of agenda we are talking about enacted. So my real concern is that we find a way to implement the changes and programs we are talking about.

MAYOR FREEDMAN:

All of us in our own cities formed alliances with businesses of all types, and yet at no meeting of various organizations that I have attended over the years have we ever before developed a strategy that would bring together those very same alliances for a national urban strategy.

MAYOR AGNOS:

I've been listening to the conversation, and I just wanted to make sure that we don't make the mistake of thinking that somehow these public/private partnerships are going to take the place of the responsibility.

I think federal and state governments have to give us what we need to do our jobs. I don't know how it is in your cities, but I've tried public/private partnerships. Unfortunately, I've found that a lot of businesses want a big building in exchange or some kind of zoning exemption or a reduction in taxes; in the end I got a 10 percent tip, and they got 90 percent of the value.

But although I may not be as sanguine as you are about partnerships, I support them where they are useful and productive, and I think we ought to have a partnership strategy, but only where they work, where they make sense.

MAYOR SCHMOKE:

The first thing to do is to clearly define the responsibilities of different levels of government for services in the cities, and to decide how each level of government influences the quality of life of people living in cities.

MAYOR GOODE:

What cities need is for the federal and state governments to deal with social and human problems in our cities, to shoulder their rightful share of the implied costs. We did not create homelessness, we did not create the problem of AIDS, we did not create the problem of drugs, and we should not be left with the burden of solving those problems alone. We did not create the economic climate facing America, and we should not be left with the issue of dealing with the problem of those who are unemployed.

MAYOR PEÑA:

An approach we can take here is to talk about partnerships, about forming a compact with the federal government in which we agree that we'll be responsible for our local economies and our infrastructure while the federal government and the states will be responsibile for welfare, health benefits, housing, and the like.

MAYOR FRASER:

It's not just the president we need to educate. We need to change public expectations that you can have government services without paying for them. I would point to children's well-being, to crime and public safety, to housing and the homeless as three recognizable priorities that most people will accept. I think we have to say that public goods are no less desirable than private goods, and that public goods that deal with children, with public safety, are more important than the second VCR or the second automobile. If we don't say it, who is going to say it?

MAYOR ABRAMSON:

It seems that our voices are simply not heard when we represent our cities. Our responsibility is to expand the base of support. We have to develop a game plan to get others singing the same tune that we're singing, especially those who are surrounding our cities and are dependent on them. The issues that we confront today are regional in nature. They're regional in terms of hazardous waste, air and water pollution, solid waste management. They're regional in terms of drugs. Certainly, drug dealers and those who steal to buy and to sell don't know the jurisdictional boundaries of the City of Louisville, where it starts and stops and when they're in the next county. If you're going to create a work force for the year 2000 and beyond, folks from the city are going to be needed to man or, excuse me, person the jobs of the future. One of the major responsibilities of this Summit will be for us to explain why it's the suburban folks' fight also; if they're not involved with us at this stage, they're ultimately going to be involved anyway as those issues permeate the rings around our cities.

MAYOR WHITE:

If we go down the tubes, these communities that ring our cities are going to go down with us. Making that clear is one way to begin to enlist some sincere assistance on the part of our suburban neighbors.

MAYOR DINKINS:

Several of you have mentioned, quite appropriately, the need for suburbia to recognize how important cities are, just as the national government needs to recognize how important cities are. I would commend to your attention the survey,[1] which shows that the people in suburbia understand how important the cities are. So I suggest respectfully that the people are ahead of government, and somehow or other we've got to get the message out to Washington that the people who live in suburbia in great numbers recognize how important the cities are, so much so that they're even willing to be taxed more highly in order to assist.

THE MAYORS SPENT SOME TIME DEVELOPING CONCRETE PROPOSALS THAT WOULD SUPPORT THE NEEDS THEY HAD SPELLED OUT. ONE OF THE MAJOR PROPOSALS, PUT FORTH BY MAYOR FLYNN AND ELABORATED ON BY MANY OF HIS COLLEAGUES, WAS TO SET FORTH A COMPETITIVE CITIES ACT.

MAYOR FLYNN:

What would a Competitive Cities Act of 1991 contain? Tax incentives for investing in our cities. New incentives for investing in research and development and minority-owned projects. Lifting the cap on tax-exempt bonds in targeted urban areas. Also a trade and economic development partnership—$500 million in funding to large cities, $250 million to small cities, and $250 million for rural areas. These are small block grants to spend for improved enterprise or economic opportunity zones. And federal contract requirements in all contracts over $10 million with for-profit or private nonprofit entities, guaranteeing that the contracting organization will establish a program of summer or after-school employment, apprenticeship programs, or mentoring for disadvantaged youth. Also, a computer corps program in which computer science graduates and professionals could instruct inner-city youths and adults in computer literacy skills.

MAYOR NORQUIST:

I think it sends out the right message, and it points to the value of cities as opposed to their problems—that has been too much in focus in the past.

MAYOR BARTHELEMY:

Yes. I like it, too. But I think one thing that we don't mention in it—I don't know how much success we'll have if we add it—is restructuring the tax laws. I think that the tax reform passed in 1986 has been detrimental to housing in the cities. If we're ever going to recapture a lot of our old housing stock, it is going to require changing that tax law.

MAYOR O'CONNOR:

I think the idea of a Competitive Cities Act is exceptional, and I like the idea of not using just direct funding but the tax code to finance some of the needs of our cities. If we could use the Moynihan bill, which is focused on aid to museums and allows taking an appreciated asset and deducting the full value, and come up with a version that substitutes, capital improvements—whether libraries, for example, or police stations—the private sector is going to be more willing to say yes, they'll give because they'll get a tax deduction and credit for helping out.

MAYOR TURNER:

The issue is not survival, it's helping cities to succeed and move forward. I think the competitive cities concept is terrific. What we are asking is the opportunity for the cities to become self-reliant—to have self-determination and be given the tools they need to become successful.

MAYOR ACEVEDO:

We need the tools of tax incentive and all the other tools to make the city self-sufficient. We should use the term "investments." We should invest in our city. But we also have immediate problems that I don't think a single city represented in this room will be able to handle by itself in the next year if we do not act now and act very, very forcefully.

MAYOR FREEDMAN:

One tool is a policy, which gives incentives to those cities that are fighting a good fight, and developing targeted types of programs in important areas such as housing, the environment, transportation, and so forth. There need to be some rewards in the system as opposed to additional penalties, as so often occurs. There has to be some loosening up on the federal level of those few dollars that flow to us so that at the local level we have the ability to put them where we need them.

MAYOR BOLEN:

Flexibility. You let every mayor in this meeting here today use whatever funds he or she can get and loosen up the strings on them, and I'll guarantee you we'll get a better bang for our buck.

MAYOR McCANN:

One of the big problems with Washington and my own state government is the programs that they mandate. They tell us that they want us to perform certain functions, certain services, and then they never clearly give us the money to provide those activities. At some point, they then cut back the funding on those programs, yet they expect us either to continue to provide the service or to do away with the service altogether. So, one of the things that we might do collectively is agree that if the federal government mandates any program to us, Washington pay.

MAYOR GREENE:

I can't support anything that says to the federal government that it should raise the income tax rates for our citizens because people in my city do not want to pay higher taxes; I think as an alternative I would like to suggest cutting spending, something all of us around this table are experts at doing.

MAYOR RILEY:

The national leadership does not talk sense to the American public. We've had to raise taxes, and I think it makes sense if America believes that the conditions in our cities are a national security interest. More money is needed, and we have to be honest with the American public and tell them so. If the case is laid out, the people will support it.

THE MAYORS INDICATED THEIR BELIEF THAT, GIVEN WHAT THE CITIES NEEDED FROM THE FEDERAL GOVERNMENT, IT WAS CRITICAL THAT THEY TRY TO MAKE THEIR VOICES HEARD IN THE NATIONAL ELECTIONS.

MAYOR NORQUIST:

We need to declare our intention to communicate with and evaluate presidential candidates, all of them, including the current president, and ask them what they're going to do to make cities function better and produce more wealth.

MAYOR KENNEY:

We should establish a theme in terms of the 1992 election warning national politicians that they must recognize that if we don't pay now, we'll pay much more later. And we need to make it clear that they cannot ignore the urban inner-city vote as they have in recent years.

MAYOR SCHEIBEL:

I think we must say that we're going to be looking at every candidate, and we're going to be a political force in the 1992 election to make sure that cities are heard.

MAYOR BRADLEY:

There was a comment about how we get our message across. I think this Summit has been an excellent jumping-off point. We've gotten a lot of media coverage, and we must not let that die. As you run your campaigns, it's repetition that finally gets the message across. We have to repeat these statements in different forums and in different conditions and by different people. I think that it is going to be up to us to organize and orchestrate that kind of image rebuilding so we can send our message to all the places it needs to go.

PAPERS

The Making of the Summit

BY RONALD BERKMAN AND JOYCE F. BROWN

In November 1990, some three dozen mayors responded to a call to come together to develop a plan that would position cities to respond to profound changes occurring in the nation and throughout the world. This article describes the planning process that resulted in the Summit and the proceedings of the Summit itself.

The Urban Summit was engineered by a planning group that included senior aides to mayors, academics, a Washington political consultant, and a group from the office of a New York City deputy mayor. Over a six-month period, we developed a concept for the meetings, polled mayors to gauge what they wanted to discuss at the Summit, organized a national planning committee consisting of mayors from around the country, conducted a national poll to explore America's attitudes about cities, formed a national university research network, and managed the complicated logistical problems involved in bringing thirty-eight mayors to New York City for the meeting.

The initial proposal for a mayoral Summit conference was delivered by Mayor David N. Dinkins in a speech before a national meeting of the U.S. Conference of Mayors in Chicago in June 1990. In the speech, Dinkins extolled the historic role of cities as generators of commerce, art, and science and warned of the consequences of a national policy that allowed cities to deteriorate socially and economically. The speech was delivered during the days when there was heady talk of a "peace dividend" that could be redirected to the resolution of domestic problems: "At this Summit, there will be more than Mayors talking to Mayors because I'm going to ask you to invite key business people from your communities. At the Summit, we'll discuss the Peace Dividend and how to plan for it and how to get it. We'll speak out, again, for the needs of our city. But we will also discuss innovative programs between business and government that can reach out to our communities—especially to our young people."

Soon after returning from Chicago, Mayor Dinkins assigned the organization of the Summit to Bill Lynch, deputy mayor for intergovernmental affairs. The mayor announced his intention to hold the Summit in October, barely five months after the original announcement in Chicago. Although no one was quite sure about the magnitude of the enterprise, most were certain that it could not be accomplished in such a short time. While Lynch recognized the severe time constraints, he was insistent that we adhere to the date announced by Dinkins. We decided on a two-day Summit from November 11 to November 13. The desire was to have a Summit with big-city mayors, but there was no universal definition of a "big city" to guide our identification of participants. In defining a population threshold for a big city, the goal was twofold: to have a widely representative sample of American cities at the meeting and to have cities that would be united by a relatively similar set of problems and concerns. The cutoff decision soon narrowed to a choice between cities with 200,000 or 300,000 residents. Using 1986 Census data, there were fewer than fifty cities with populations exceeding 300,000 and more than seventy-five cities with populations exceeding 200,000. The planning group recommended that a larger number and diversity of cities would enhance the potential impact of the meeting, and Mayor Dinkins accepted that all cities with populations greater than 200,000, including cities in Puerto Rico, be invited to participate in the Summit.

We then assembled a group of mayors to serve as a Planning Committee for the Summit. The goal was to have a Planning Committee that was regionally, demographically, and politically representative. The mayors serving as presidents of the National League of Cities and U.S. Conference of Mayors were also invited to serve on the Planning Committee. Each of the mayoral designees to the Planning Committee was personally called by Mayor Dinkins, who reviewed the preliminary plan for the meeting, solicited feedback from the mayors, and secured their commitment to participate.*

Anticipating the need to clarify the purpose of the Summit for the mayors who agreed to serve on the Planning Committee, the Lynch group prepared a "concept paper" describing some of its potential themes and goals. It was sent to all the mayors for review and became the focus for

---

* Members of the Planning Committee:

Raymond Flynn,	Boston
Richard Daley,	Chicago
Federico Peña,	Denver
Kathy Whitmire,	Houston
Tom Bradley,	Los Angeles
Jerry Abramson,	Louisville
David Dinkins,	New York City
Norman Rice,	Seattle
Robert Isaacs,	Colorado Springs (president, U.S. Conference of Mayors)
Bob Boland,	San Antonio (president, National League of Cities)

the first national Planning Committee meeting. The goals outlined in the concept paper included:

▲ forming a stronger and more directed network among big-city mayors as a basis for collaboration on common interests and public policy

▲ exploring existing relationships between city constituencies (business, labor, community groups) in pursuit of new strategies for cooperation in economic and social development

▲ developing an "Urban Compact" embodying a new urban agenda

▲ constructing a program to make the condition of urban America a priority for state and federal government policymakers and the budgets they draft

▲ developing a national research and public opinion network focused on cities

The first formal meeting of the national Planning Committee was held on August 13, 1990, at Gracie Mansion, the official residence of the mayor of New York City. Mayors were represented by deputy mayors or senior staff with responsibility for the project. There were two distinct approaches to the Summit advocated at this first meeting. One was to use the Summit to discuss and promote solutions for the most serious problems facing American cities—education, health care, drugs, crime, and the like. The supporters of this approach felt that it was disingenuous to have a meeting of urban mayors that did not address the problems that each, to varying degrees, had to confront. Another group of cities endorsed the implicit direction outlined in the concept paper, which emphasized the need for cities to plan more effectively, organize coalitions, and foster a popular appreciation for their economic, social, and cultural values. While the first meeting did not produce an unequivocal commitment to one of these approaches, majority sentiment favored the latter direction.

Equally important was the lively discussion of the "politics" of the meeting. The debate centered on the degree of emphasis that should be placed on using the meeting to make a strong public plea for increased state and federal assistance. There was strong resistance to using what was commonly called the "tin cup approach," which might be interpreted by the media as simply another call for more funding. Yet the contemporary problems of the cities are inextricably linked to the mounting withdrawal of state and federal tax revenue during the past decade. The Planning

Committee never resolved the issue. However, questions on what the mayors wanted from the meeting was introduced repeatedly by the press and was an important consideration in how much the mayors addressed the substantive questions.

Within the Planning Committee, there was unanticipated resistance to the idea, originally proposed by Mayor Dinkins, that the Summit include representatives of the business community from participating cities. Again and again, the members of the Planning Committee extolled the Summit as a unique opportunity for a relatively small number of mayors to have a direct dialogue, something that rarely occurs in the large meetings of the national organizations. While there was enthusiasm for the prospect of a meeting between mayors and business executives, the majority of the committee believed that a dialogue between mayors should precede a meeting with business.

The creation of the Planning Committee was an important step in broadening the constituency and enlarging input into the planning process. Yet there were many cities that were to be invited and would play no direct role in planning. To provide this group of cities with a means to influence the process, the Planning Committee endorsed a survey to determine what the mayors wanted to discuss. The questionnaire was derived from the themes in the concept paper and expanded to reflect issues proposed by members of the Planning Committee.

The August meetings of the Planning Committee, a brainstorming session with academics and the responses of the mayors to the questionnaire, provided a general sense of the issues that would likely be included in the Summit. There were three overarching categories for discussion.

▲ **The Global Economy**—How is the nature of a city's economy changed by globalization? How can cities restructure their economy to effectively participate in a new economic order?

▲ **Partnership**—What public and private partnerships are needed to advance economic and social development?

▲ **Fiscal Challenges**—How can cities redirect national spending and tax policy and better utilize existing resources?

It was necessary at this stage to assemble a research team and begin the developmental process. The research group consisted of faculty from the CUNY Graduate Center, academics in various cities identified by mayors, a research team from the N.Y.-N.J. Port Authority, and a half dozen graduate students. At first, we envisioned a briefing book for the Summit of considerable girth and substance, containing a well-integrated blend of data, case studies, scholarly research, and analysis. The briefing book would come in two versions: a digest that could be quickly absorbed by the participants and a larger volume that could be used for later reference. All the research material would be indexed to the various topics on the agenda so that a mayor could quickly flip to the pertinent section for additional information. In addition to this already robust plan, we envisioned completing original research on the voting patterns of urban and suburban residents, conducting a national poll and a survey of Congress. In time, the research group came to recognize that there were insufficient resources, inadequate time, and less than a pressing need for this level of research.

A separate group of survey researchers assembled to plan for two surveys that the Planning Committee had decided to pursue. A survey of national attitudes about cities was necessary to fill a void in our knowledge about how Americans use cities and how they feel about particular city issues. A thorough search of the existing survey research bibliographies produced very little data on Americans' attitudes toward cities. Most of the existing surveys contained data on the cities that respondents felt had the most attractive women, the best food, the best parks, and so forth. To develop some evidence about how suburban residents used their neighboring city and about their views concerning a set of urban social, economic, and political issues, the City University of New York developed a questionnaire and commissioned an established survey research firm to conduct the survey. (The results of this study are analyzed in detail in the paper beginning on page 37 in this volume.)

In the course of the many discussions of Congress, we began to realize that we also lacked any "hard" data on congressional attitudes toward cities. Cities no longer sent a majority of the House to Washington or controlled most of the important levers of congressional power. It was evident that members from urban districts, even if they voted as a block, could not produce the votes needed to pass legislation advantageous to cities. Thus, the urban delegations were going to have to build coalitions with suburban and rural members. There was very little evidence to indicate the types of issues around which such coalitions could form. The second proposed survey was to begin the process of identifying such issues. However, such a survey would be labor-intensive and require personal interviews with congressional members. These considerations precluded us from being able to design and complete it in time for the Summit. It remains, however, an important area for investigation.

At the Planning Committee meeting on September 10, 1990, two months prior to the event, a number of important issues moved closer to resolution. The Summit would have three meetings on the first day, organized around each of the central topics outlined in the concept paper (global competitiveness, partnerships, fiscal challenges) and a meeting on the following day to ratify a compact. The September planning session provided the first opportunity to review a draft of the urban compact, containing a description of particular themes, some data analyses, and recommendations for action. Prompted by the realization that the compact represented the final product of the Summit, the group's attention became fixed on the document. There was a protracted and inconclusive discussion of the form and content of the compact. Representatives of four cities agreed to meet in Washington, consider all the suggestions for revision, produce a new draft of the document, and circulate it to the committee.

A considerable portion of the September meeting was consumed by debate on how to handle the media. This discussion was sharply focused and intensely argued, no doubt as a result of the committee members' recognition of the pivotal role of the media in assigning importance to the event. (See the paper beginning on page 87 in this volume.) The most critical decision was whether to admit journalists into the actual meetings of the mayors. Admission of the media would likely constrain free exchange among the mayors; the question was whether the enhanced exposure was worth the sacrifice. The group decided that it was not. Press would be excluded from the four working sessions but provided with opportunities to question the chairs of the meeting and the other mayors at the conclusion of each session. Two formal press conferences were scheduled, an initial one to introduce the purpose of the Summit and one following the final meeting to present the completed urban compact. The decision to exclude media from the actual meetings strengthened the definition of the meeting as a serious collaboration of America's big-city mayors.

On September 25, the representatives of four cities met in Washington as scheduled to draft a compact from the various revisions submitted by members of the Planning Committee. After two days of meetings, the group realized that the revised compact would not be a final statement of the Summit, but a broader document from which a final statement would be crafted.

The final meeting of the Planning Committee on October 22 revealed considerable disagreement on the form, direction, scope, and substance of the revised compact. Given the limits of time, the group decided to create three subgroups to review and rewrite the sections on competitiveness, partnerships, and fiscal challenges. Although there was very little actual rewriting done in the groups, there was general agreement on a design for a final document.

The October Planning Committee meeting set the terms of the Summit. All of the closed sessions would be chaired by two mayors, who would be asked to bring the group toward a consensus on the recommendations, or "action items," as they are called in the compact. There would be no outside speakers or formal presentations by experts. Each of the session chairs would be permitted a five-minute opening statement. One of the academics invited to the Summit by a mayor on the Planning Committee would be asked to serve as a recorder for each of the sessions and communicate the record of the proceedings to the drafting committee. A final morning session was scheduled to review and ratify the draft.

Over the next two weeks, there were intensive communications about the content and direction of the compact briefing papers. Some of the Planning Committee advocated editorial changes, but the bulk of the suggestions were political in nature. During this period, there was an unsuccessful effort to organize sentiment in favor of abandoning the idea of creating a compact or briefing papers and allowing the mayors to simply sit down at the table and discuss anything they wanted. There was another move to scrap the formula of narrative and "action items" in favor of a document that would contain resolutions that could be voted up or down. This idea was slightly more popular than the idea to abandon the compact completely, but could not gather a critical mass of support. Most of the attention centered on the various "action items" that would be presented to the mayors for consideration. Agreement on a final draft of the briefing papers was reached hours prior to the deadline for the Summit material to go to press. It was understood that mayors would be free to add to or delete any of the language in the document during the course of the meetings.

On the first day of the Summit, the mayors chairing particular sessions, with a few exceptions, tended to focus attention on the overall themes and issues, straying some distance from the actual words in the draft document. Fortunately, the recorders were very effective in relating the discussion to both the narrative and "action item" sections of the document.

Any member of the Planning Committee who so desired was invited to participate in drafting the final compact. Virtually all the members of the Planning Committee, including the representatives of the U.S. Conference of Mayors and National League of Cities participated in all or part of the twelve-hour session. Several mayoral representatives from cities not on the Planning Committee found their way into the ostensibly "closed-door" session.

The drafting committee began its work directly after the conclusion of the morning meetings. Most of the participants worked from the end of the last afternoon meeting until the final touches were put on the compact at 3:00 a.m. on the following morning. At times, small groups worked on drafts of the document as a whole or on particular sections, but the drafts were always reviewed by all the members. The realization that there was no alternative to reaching agreement provided sufficient incentive for cooperation.

Copies of "In the National Interest" were delivered to each mayor by 7:00 a.m. on the second morning of the Summit, providing an opportunity for them to review the document before the 9:00 a.m. session. At noon, the mayors were scheduled to appear at a press conference and release the final report. Consequently, there were three hours in which to entertain the changes proposed by mayors, reach consensus, and reproduce a revised compact.

From the beginning of the planning process, this session was seen as the most crucial and potentially the most problematic. Given the need to work through the document with the whole group, the Planning Committee decided to choose mayoral chairs with experience in running city council sessions. Accustomed to moving policy and legislation through councils, the mayors presiding over the concluding session did a remarkable job of reviewing, revising, and modifying the document in just under three hours. Only once in the course of three hours of amendments, additions, deletions, and editorial comments was it necessary to call for a vote of the group. In all other instances, the chairs were able to fashion a remedy that satisfied all the mayors.

The final press conference featured the mayors who participated. There was no duplication in the messages conveyed—each mayor managed to find a unique theme or wrinkle that amplified the points made by other mayors. Although the mayors were asked a stock repertoire of hostile questions on federal aid, budgeting, the recession, they responded with passion and conviction. Two days of open communications with colleagues who understood the nature of the problems and the magnitude of the challenges had produced a powerful coalition of spokespersons for urban America.

In the months following the Summit, the Planning Committee continued to meet to act upon the agenda articulated in "In the National Interest." In May, a group of eight mayors met with the leadership of Congress and fifty members to explain the legislation advocated at the Summit. Senator Kennedy announced the introduction of a bill that would make Head Start an entitlement for all children, an idea that he announced he had "stolen" from the Summit. Congressmen Sheas, McDermott, and Foglietta announced the formation of a congressional Urban Caucus, endorsed by the Summit. The Planning Committee met with leaders from the national business community to draft a plan for a "corporate summit," the national meeting of corporate leaders and mayors originally envisioned by Mayor Dinkins.

The Summit has raised the level of public and political awareness about the importance of cities and the magnitude of the problems they face in a period of political and economic transformation. However, it was only the beginning of what must be a protracted campaign to focus America's attention on the nature of our domestic challenges and the tremendous costs that we will pay if we allow them to go unmet.

AMERICANS AND THEIR CITIES: SOLICITUDE AND SUPPORT

A REPORT TO

THE URBAN SUMMIT—1990

Prepared by

The Robert F. Wagner, Sr. Institute
Graduate Center
City University of New York
Dr. Arthur S. Goldberg, Research Director

With the Assistance of

Schulman, Ronca & Bucuvalas, Inc.
New York, New York

BACKGROUND

This study of American perceptions of cities was undertaken to discover whether cities live in an adversarial relationship with the rest of the nation. The nature of today's urban problems (drugs, AIDS, homelessness, crime), the media coverage of these problems, and the painfully slow and limited response of the federal government suggest that such an adversarial relationship may indeed be the case. In particular, we wanted to answer two questions:

- ▲ Do those who live within and those who live outside of America's hundred largest cities share common perceptions about the problems challenging these cities?

- ▲ Are nonurban residents willing to increase federal assistance in order to deal with urban problems, even if it means higher taxes?

To answer these questions, we conducted a nationwide, random-digit-dial telephone survey during October 1990.[1] Twenty-one percent of the resulting sample lived in one of the hundred largest cities in the United States, and 79% lived outside of those cities. These proportions closely conform to U.S. Census estimates. At the 95% statistical confidence level, our data had a level of precision of +/-3% for the entire sample, +/-3.5% for the out-of-city subsample, and +/-8% for the in-city subsample.

In order to investigate the attitudes of city and out-of-city residents, we asked respondents to rate the seriousness of the following problems: drugs; crime; AIDS; homelessness; teenage pregnancy; school dropout rate; lack of job skills; unemployment; and economic decline. We also asked out-of-city respondents to rate their willingness to be taxed to help the cities with each of the following problems: housing for the poor; AIDS prevention and treatment; public schools; child health care; drug rehabilitation; job training; roads, buildings, and other infrastructure; law enforcement; preschool programs; prenatal care; middle-income housing; and mass transit.[2]

An important element of our research design was the specification of a "reference city" for each respondent. Too often, the discussion of cities focuses upon some abstraction like "the city" or "urban America." Such terminology in a survey has great potential for conjuring up in the mind of the respondent only our very largest cities—New York City, Los

---

[1]We conducted a stratified, multistage cluster sample survey (n = 1199) during the period October 3–17, 1990. The telephone survey was conducted by Schulman, Ronca & Bucuvalas, Inc., a national marketing firm based in New York City. The survey design and data analysis were performed at the Wagner Institute of the Graduate Center of City University of New York.

[2]Respondents were asked about these issues in a random order.

Angeles, Chicago, and such—of which the respondent may have had little or no experience. Since urban problems are by no means confined to our very largest cities, and because we wanted to give our respondents the opportunity to respond to cities they were more or less familiar with, we avoided the use of such abstractions in our questions. Instead, we focused on the hundred largest cities in the United States, and directed the respondent to answer questions about the city in which he or she lived (if that was one of the hundred largest) or the city in the hundred largest that was most important to the respondent.

We offered our out-of-city respondents a choice of the three closest cities in the hundred largest. The respondent was then asked to select the city that was "most important to your household." Thus, a respondent in Kerrville, Texas, was not asked to focus on New York City, Chicago, or Los Angeles but was instead asked to talk about San Antonio, Austin, or Corpus Christi. Similarly, the respondent in Pendelton, Indiana, was asked to choose from among Indianapolis, Cincinnati, and Dayton, and the respondent in West Boylston, Massachusetts, was asked to choose from among Boston, Yonkers, and New York City.

Eight percent of our respondents lived in one of the nation's seven largest cities and discussed those cities; 17% of our respondents both lived outside of our hundred largest cities and selected one of the seven largest U.S. cities as being most important to their household; 16% of our respondents both lived outside of our one hundred largest cities and selected a city in the 8th–20th rank by size as the focus of discussion; and so forth. The result is a reasonable out-of-city sample base discussing each of the four size ranks of city, and a set of responses that are informed by reference to an actual city rather than an abstract concept.

THE CENTRALITY OF CITIES

Before discussing our central findings, it is worth considering the geographic relationship between American citizens and their hundred largest cities and how it affects popular perceptions.

First, it is simply not the case that our cities are at some great remove from the mass of our citizens. Some 21% of our population live in our hundred largest cities, another 22% live within 20 miles, and another 22% live within 21–60 miles. Thus, 65% of our citizens live either in one of our major cities or within an hour or two drive from one of them.

Second, it is simply not the case that our major cities—even the largest of them—are abhorred by either those who live in them or those outside. As can be seen in Figure 1:

> ▲ When in-city respondents were asked how they feel about the city in which they live, 82% said they like it, and, of those, 76% said that they like it a lot.

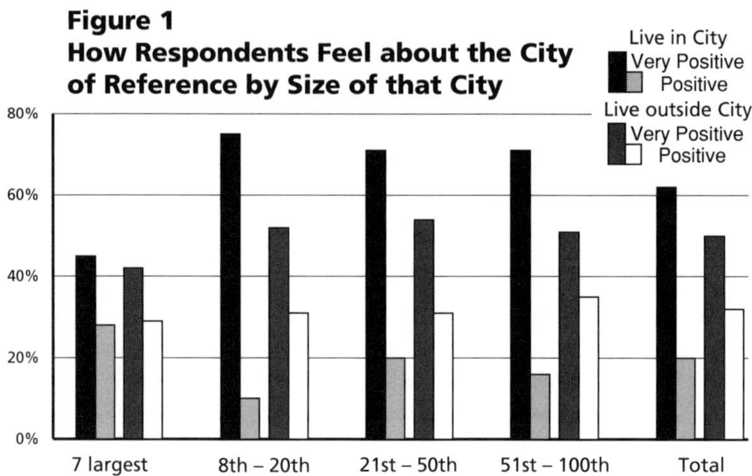

- ▲ When those who live in one of the seven largest cities were asked this, 73% said they like it, and, of those, 62% said they like it a lot.

- ▲ When out-of-city respondents were asked how they felt about the city they had selected for discussion, 82% said they like it, and, of those, 61% said they like it a lot.

- ▲ Among those out-of-city respondents for whom the city selected for discussion was one of the seven largest, 71% said that they like it, and, of those, 37% said that they like it a lot.

Thus, while one can argue from these data that the very largest cities engender somewhat less affection than do other cities, it should be kept in mind that, in general, cities—including even our largest cities—are viewed positively by the citizenry.

THE SERIOUSNESS OF URBAN PROBLEMS

The data suggest that, problem by problem, in-city and out-of-city respondents regard any given problem as serious to very much the same extent. This is evident in Figure 2, where in-city and out-of-city respondents are compared on how seriously each views a specified problem in the city under discussion.

- ▲ Those who live in cities and those outside do not have incompatible images of the same world. The problems of our cities appear about equally ominous to both groups.

However, the perceived seriousness does vary by size of city, both for those in the cities and for those outside of them. Figure 3 reveals some important differences between in-city and out-of-city respondents with respect to certain problems in the seven largest cities.

- ▲ Those who live in the seven largest cities regard almost all of the problems of their cities as "very serious" to a greater extent than do out-of-city respondents who discuss those same cities. However, this is particularly true in the case of AIDS and homelessness.

So while there is a common view, those with the most intense exposure to problems that have developed only in the past several years view them with somewhat greater urgency.

WILLINGNESS TO PROVIDE FUNDING

Figure 4 shows that there is substantial willingness to help pay for certain programs among those who do not live in the cities. There is majority support for almost all of the programs in question. Indeed, there is substantial (60%) to massive (74%) support for almost all "helping" programs—especially the following:

- ▲ Housing for the poor (74%)
- ▲ AIDS prevention (72%)
- ▲ AIDS treatment (71%)

What is perhaps most remarkable about this willingness to provide funding is that, for any given program, it varies only slightly by size of the city being discussed or by region of the country.

- ▲ Thus, respondents from outside the very largest cities, in spite of their lesser affection for the city, seem as willing as those who live outside smaller cities to provide money for program support.

- ▲ Moreover, whether one is talking about a heavily urbanized region, such as the Northeast, or a much less urbanized region, such as the South, support for any given program is, with few exceptions, quite similar. Notable exceptions to this are the Midwest on housing for the poor, and the Northeast on AIDS and on child health care. In each of these instances the region is notably more supportive.

While support among out-of-city respondents tends to be fairly uniform for any given program, there are two interesting dimensions revealing a pattern of consistent variation.

- ▲ When these data are analyzed by gender, it becomes evident that women are consistently more supportive of people-oriented programs than are men, and that men are somewhat more supportive of "bricks and mortar" programs than are women. But

Figure 2
Perceived Seriousness of Problems in City
by Respondent's Location

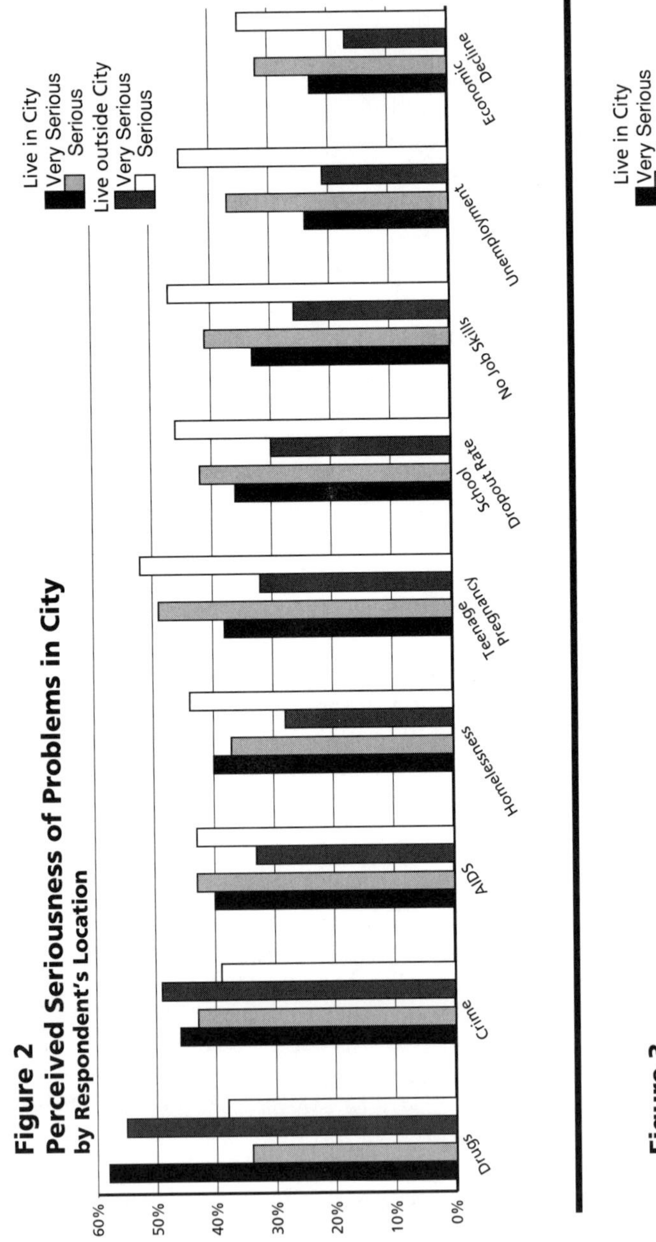

Figure 3
Perceived Seriousness of Problems in City
by Size of City – Respondents in and outside of City

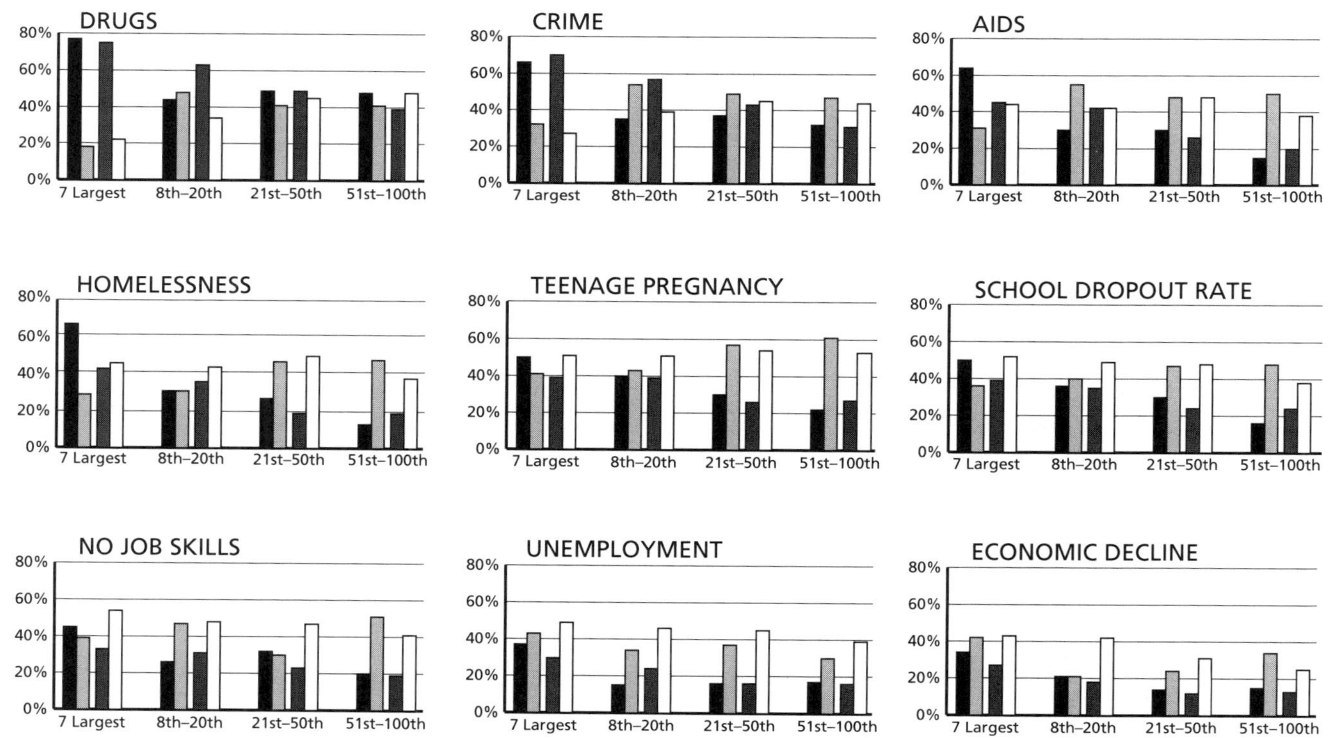
DRUGS
CRIME
AIDS
HOMELESSNESS
TEENAGE PREGNANCY
SCHOOL DROPOUT RATE
NO JOB SKILLS
UNEMPLOYMENT
ECONOMIC DECLINE
7 Largest
8th–20th
21st–50th
51st–100th
0%
20%
40%
60%
80%

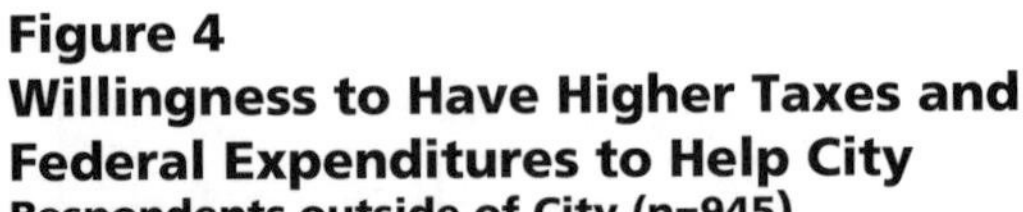

Figure 4
Willingness to Have Higher Taxes and
Federal Expenditures to Help City
Respondents outside of City (n=945)

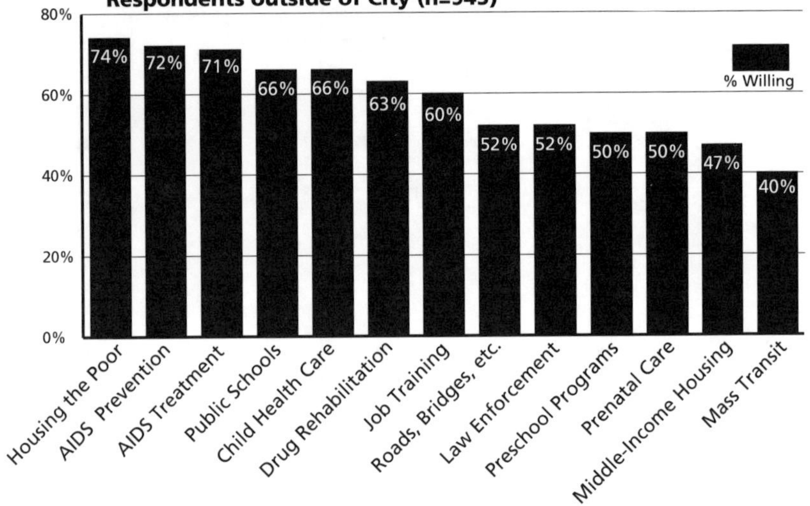

Figure 5
Willingness to Have Higher Taxes and
Federal Expenditures to Help City, by Income
Respondents outside of City (n=945)

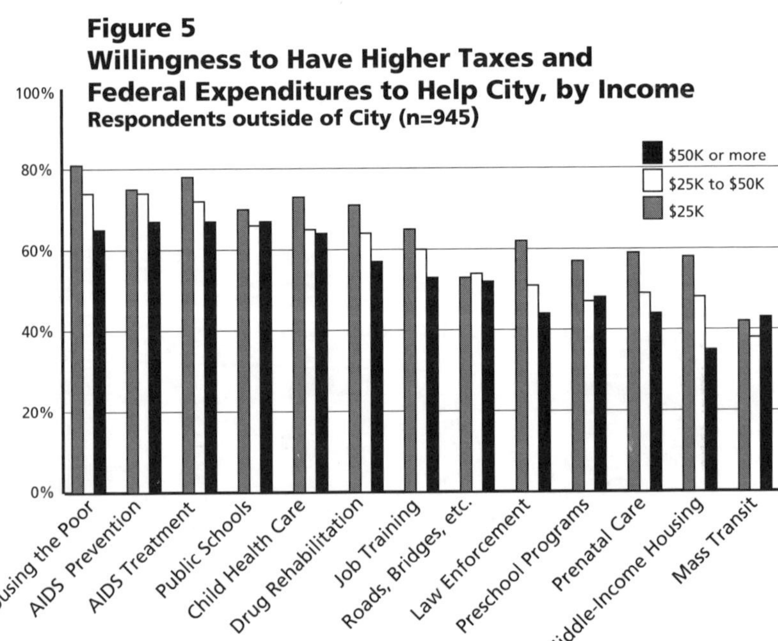

although these differences occasionally run as high as 18 percentage points, there are no massive polarizations.

▲ Looking at the data by household income (Figure 5), one finds that on all programs other than "bricks and mortar" projects, those with the highest household incomes are apt to be substantially less supportive than are those with the lowest household incomes.

Since the higher income classes would likely experience the larger tax increase to pay for these programs, this should not be altogether surprising. Note, however, that even in the highest household income category there is majority support for eight of thirteen programs, and support in excess of 60% for five of them.

OTHER FINDINGS

Among our respondents there is a recognized interdependence between city and suburban regions. Focusing upon the 22% of Americans who do not live in one of the nation's hundred largest cities but who do live within 20 miles of one of them, we found that:

▲ 46% of the respondents' households have at least one member who works in the city;

▲ 67% depend upon that city for major medical services;

▲ 43% have household members who either currently attend (directly or through one of its branches) an institution of higher learning based in that city or anticipate doing so within five years;

▲ 66% own their own homes, and almost half (46%) of those homeowners believe that a long-term economic decline in the city would reduce the market value of their homes.

CONCLUSION

By and large, Americans—including those who do not live in major cities—are aware of, concerned about, and willing to help address the problems that challenge cities. Clearly, there is not uniform support across all issues, nor is there unanimous support on any. However, in a nation where a presidential candidate receiving 60% of the vote is considered to have won by a "landslide," and in which presidential approval ratings above 60% are rare, the fact that there are absolute majorities of nonurbanites willing to have their taxes increased in order to help the cities strongly suggests that this is not an "us versus them" situation, that those living beyond city limits recognize their own welfare is in some way bound up with the health of urban America.

The Mayors and the Federal System

BY FRANCES FOX PIVEN

A public convening of big-city mayors to formulate an "urban platform" is inevitably an effort to influence national opinion and policy. However much they may eschew the characterization, the mayors are cast as national advocates for urban constituencies. There are, I will argue, good reasons for this. Moreover, a glance backward across the twentieth century suggests the mayors have played this role before, especially during periods of fiscal and political stress in the cities. I want in this paper to consider the distinctive features of the American political system that sometimes propel the mayors to become urban lobbyists within the federal edifice.

National policies necessarily have large and complex consequences on localities, some of them perverse. But in the American federal system, it falls to local governments to cope with many of these consequences. In principle, this disjunction between policy causes and policy consequences might be overcome by centralized forms of political organization, particularly by strong national political parties capable of articulating broad constituency interests and coordinating the responses of different governmental actors. In actuality, however, fragmented government structures have also encouraged fragmented politics, inhibiting the connections between national policies and local problems. Only under extraordinary conditions of fiscal and political crisis, when local problems become overwhelming, has this disjunction sometimes been overcome. And when it has, big-city mayors have played a large role in bringing the problems of their local constituencies into the arena of national politics and policy.

FEDERALISM AND POLICYMAKING STRUCTURES

Despite the tangle of interpenetrating and overlapping authorities, it is fair to generalize that federalism has resulted in a kind of division of labor in the realm of policy and politics. Policies with larger scope, which are often the policies likely to fix the parameters of economic and social development for the nation and its localities, tend to be set at the national level. Thus, from the beginnings of the republic, currency and tariff policy, internal trade, territorial expansion, immigration, foreign relations, and military capabilities were the special province of the national government. Later, the federal government also came to play a large role in promoting railroad development, regulating industrial competition, and mediating labor relations. Of course, for a long time, the states were also important players in economic development, particularly through policies that established the basic legal framework for the corporation and suppressed labor militancy, and also through infrastructure development. But over time, and especially as markets for capital, goods, and labor became national markets, federal policies became steadily more important. Moreover, contemporary rhetoric about reduced government notwithstanding, the rise of international markets ensures that the national government will play a steadily larger role in shaping the character of domestic economic activity, and all the aspects of social and political life that depend on it.

The large role of national government is not unusual for a modern, industrialized democracy. Rather, the activity, as well as the sheer number, of subnational governments distinguished the American federal system. The vitality of local governments sprang from their performance of many important functions, usually with a good deal of autonomy and with revenue-raising responsibilities to match that autonomy. Localities ran the schools, cared for the indigent, policed the streets, and provided an array of local services essential to daily life. The bounds and the scale of local government activity were very much a reflection of broader patterns of economic and social development shaped largely at higher levels of authority. In this way, a potentially conflictual dynamic developed between centralizing and decentralizing tendencies within the federal system.

FEDERALISM AND POLITICS

Governmental structures not only register and respond to political influence; they also help to shape political influence, by creating new political resources and delineating the processes through which these resources are used to try to exercise influence. A constitutionally federated government fostered a segmentation or layering of American political life, simultaneously creating centralized national arenas of organization and influence and fostering a distinctively vigorous decentralized politics.

The basic outlines of the federal system were laid down by the Constitution. The political motives of the Founders have been subject to endless scrutiny and debate. Analysts have variously attributed the centralization of certain powers to political, or economic, or military concerns, to the threat of insurgency represented by Shay's rebellion, to the threat represented by radical state legislative initiatives regarding currency and debt, or to the threat of military aggression from expansionary European powers once the colonies had been stripped of the British military presence.

In retrospect, however, the decentralizing features of the Constitution turned out to be as important as the centralizing features in creating the distinctive politics of the federal system. The military and economic concerns propelling the creation of a central government were counterbalanced by arrangements that protected the sharply diverse economies of the thirteen former colonies from undue interference by central authority, as in the compromise over slavery. The more general compromise was to structurally decentralize governmental power. This was done in two ways. First, the authority of the new national government was limited to constitutionally specified policies, leaving an enormous reservoir of unspecified power to the state governments and the local governments chartered by state legislatures. Second, the system of electoral representation in the national government gave weight to regions as opposed to persons in the design of an upper chamber of the legislature, the Senate, and the electoral college for the selection of a president.

In fact, the United States is only one among many nations that came into existence through an initial compact for federation among regional governmental powers. Elsewhere, however, these regional authorities gradually lost ground to an enlarging central government. In the United States, while the scope of national government power has certainly increased, a vigorous federalism persists because American politics has developed in a way that is intimately intertwined with and dependent on fragmented policy structures. In part this is a reflection of the continuing centrifugal pressures of political interests lodged in diverse regional economies, especially economies organized around territorially based resources. These sorts of regional economic interests had impelled the compromises between national and subnational policy authority embedded in the Constitution, and the arrangements persisted in part because regional economic diversity and the sectional interests it generated persisted.

Diverse sectional economic interests were not, however, the only political support for fragmented policy structures. Federalism was also sustained by a fragmented and decentralized party system, which reinforced the fragmented and decentralized federal arrangements that shaped them in the first place.

To explain this point requires a few words about the political role of mass parties in a democratic polity. It is widely agreed that the potential for democratic political influence in modern nations depends on the activities of political parties that mediate the relationship between citizens and government. It is political parties that presumably organize popular political hopes and discontents, generating coherent platform and candidate alternatives and mobilizing citizen-voters around those alternatives. These activities of political parties are generally taken to be crucial to democratic politics because they make possible the aggregation of votes without which citizens are atomized and therefore without influence. But the fragmented American governmental structure has worked to make our political parties uniquely ineffective in filling what Dennis Wrong has called this "creative, synthesizing" role.

A decentralized policymaking system means that subnational governments attract the efforts of state and local parties striving to win control over these levels of government. And when elections are won, the relatively autonomous authority and resources of these subnational governments in turn sustain relatively autonomous party groupings over time. To be sure, decentralization is not the only reason for the uniquely loose American party system. The parties were also weakened by the labyrinthine internal structure of national government, as E. E. Schattschneider has pointed out, as well as by the weight given sectional interests in national representational arrangements. Whatever the causes, instead of developing into truly national parties, the American parties were and remain congeries of state and local parties, together with the candidate-based organizations that have recently become important. These groups periodically come together in flimsy alliances for the purpose of contesting elections, which means bidding for control over the positions in a multilayered and internally divided government structure.

But these diverse alliances under a party banner cannot do what parties elsewhere often do to nationalize and unify the terms of popular political participation. National parties generate program alternatives, project leaders mobilize voters to support those alternatives and leaders, and then hold elected officials at all levels of government accountable to national party commitments. This is the way that voters, in contrast to interest groups, exert influence.

There is an irony in the American pattern of political development. Radical democrats at the time of the struggle over the Constitution were wary of ceding state powers to a national government, believing that democratic representation was only effective when voters could maintain close surveillance of their representatives and recall them quickly. A national government, by contrast, would necessarily be remote and inaccessible, and therefore the easy prey of elites. There were good reasons for such fears at the time. The Constitution-makers *were* elites, and they were motivated to create a national government in part by their fear of radical currents in some of the state legislatures. Still, the critique of centralization and the local vision of democratic governance that the radical democrats developed turned out to be far too simple, not only because they failed to cope with the centralizing realities of modern life, but because they could not imagine the role of political parties. It was not centralization but the localism embodied in federal arrangements that ultimately weakened democratic politics, by inhibiting the development of national parties that might make mere voters, including the great concentrations of urban voters, more effective.

A decentralized party system in turn cleared the path for the unfettered sectional and interest group politics that has always flourished in the United States. Interest groups could operate in the several branches of government, or at different levels of government, to promote the policies they favored or to block the policies they opposed. Had strong parties emerged, they would have exerted discipline over these diverse parts of government. But since the very structural arrangements that exposed government to well-organized interests also ensured the disorganization of the parties, there was little resistance from the parties to sectional and interest group demands.

THE MAYORS AND THE NATIONALIZATION OF POLITICS

In the twentieth century, this segmented political system began to break down, and mayors were important agents of the transformation. Under the impact of wrenching economic and social disturbances, urban popular discontent began to overwhelm the container of localism and make its mark on national politics. The 1930s and 1960s were critical periods, and in each period, the mayors came to play a large role in the politics of the federal system. Pressed by mounting unrest in their own jurisdictions, and by the fiscal strains of trying to deal with the disturbances, the mayors emerged in national forums to articulate the problems of the cities and to press for national action. The result in each case was a period of reform that gave rise to exceptional innovations in American public policy, a broadening of American political culture, and at least steps toward the development of national parties.

When the Great Depression began, there were no national social welfare programs in the United States. In this respect, we were backward: Bismarck inaugurated the first such programs in Germany some fifty years earlier, and these had been widely imitated in Europe. Moreover, even after several years of economic calamity, federal aid to the cities was negligible. Total federal grants to the local governments came to only $232 million.

City officials confronted the economic disaster, and the waves of popular protest it stimulated, more or less alone. As unemployment spread, urban demonstrators began to demand "bread or wages." The mayors at first fumbled with ad hoc schemes to organize food donations to the hungry or to dun city employees for contributions, or they solicited philanthropists for the funds to give temporary work to the unemployed. Meanwhile, even as the bread lines grew, city revenues plummeted, and cities tried to float bonds to pay for relief. By the winter of 1931–32, many municipalities were on the edge of fiscal collapse. Some had stopped paying their employees, many cut back public services, and others simply defaulted on their bonds. Under these conditions, the mayors became ardent lobbyists for a historic change, urging the federal government to take rapid measures to aid the cities in meeting the calamity. In Chicago, where half the work force was unemployed, Mayor Anton Cermak pleaded for federal aid now, rather than federal troops later.

The epochal emergency relief program that followed in the spring of 1933 was the first of a series of federal programs that established the framework for contemporary American social policy. Meanwhile, the U.S. Conference of Mayors was formed to provide a continuing vehicle for the articulation of urban interests. By the time the decade drew to a close, the American federal system had been transformed. Not only had a range of new programs been inaugurated by the national government to deal with social problems, but the idea of a national responsibility for what were previously considered local problems had been established.

Similar upheavals occurred in the 1960s. This time, the disturbances were set in motion by the massive exodus of blacks from the South and their migration to the big cities, where small black communities established earlier provided some kind of haven. In the cities, blacks gained voting rights and some measure of political power, but they also suffered the poverty and disorganization that resulted from the wrenching displacement from sharecropping to an urban economy. Further, the growing black population of the cities was fiercely resented by resident white majorities, particularly as blacks spilled over into white neighborhoods and white schools. Ultimately the resulting tensions escaped the boundaries of local politics as blacks became increasingly insurgent. Following the example of the civil rights movement, they addressed their grievances to national government. Mayors tried to cope with these contradictory pressures by simultaneously expanding municipal jobs and services, and by adding their voices to the demands for federal relief from the growing strains on city budgets as a consequence of the unrest. In response, federal aid to the cities rose rapidly, from about $10 billion in 1960 to $26 billion in 1970, and a range of federal programs that make a large difference in the lives of city dwellers were expanded.

A good many observers look back on the policy changes of the 1960s with a jaundiced eye, noting that despite the new and expanded federal programs, neither poverty nor racism seems to have been cured. This is of course true. But the implication that the programs were ineffective does not follow. Rather, it can be said that these modest programs were hardly sufficient to overcome the deep imprint of racism in American life, or to override the economic trends that were increasing economic and racial polarization. (Until the cutbacks of the 1980s, the programs did indeed at least partly offset those trends.) Given these limitations, the expansion of the American social welfare system during the 1960s to include medical insurance for the old and many of the poor, nutritional benefits, more subsidized housing, and somewhat improved income-main-tenance programs, especially for the disabled and the aged, should be taken as a large step forward. Moreover, it was a period of policy cre-ativity that generated entirely new forms of federal intervention, such as Community Action, Head Start, and the Legal Services programs, with some remarkable results.

A good deal of this progress was reversed under the Reagan admin-istration in the 1980s. The political reasons are evident; the Democratic administrations of the 1930s and 1960s that introduced or expanded social programs were vulnerable to the voters of the big cities. The Reagan admin-istration owed little politically to these voters or to their mayors, and was thus freer to slash the programs that aided cities. Accordingly, sharp cuts were made—and even sharper cuts attempted—in a range of social wel-fare programs, even in the teeth of the recession of 1981–82, when the cities of the industrial belt were reeling from the precipitous contrac-tion of manufacturing. Cuts in grants-in-aid for infrastructure also fell harder on cities in the industrial belt. Overall, the federal share of local revenues fell from 9 percent in 1978 to 4.2 percent in 1987.

The Republican administrations of the 1980s also set about trying to restore the segmented pattern of an earlier federalism, centralizing the policies and politics that shape economic and social development while decentralizing the policies and politics that cope with its effects. Proposals for a "New Federalism," along with the turn to block grants, were an attempt to reverse the trend toward nationalization of social welfare programs. The Bush administration has persisted in this strategy, targeting for attempted cutbacks mainly programs that serve the poor and propos-ing to consolidate welfare, food stamps, Medicaid, and the Community Development Block Grant into a huge block grant that would be turned over to to the states to spend as they wish.

The Urban Summit can be seen as an effort to point attention to the irrationalities that result from a federal system that separates respon-sibility for the policies that create urban problems from the policies need-ed to deal with them. It is also an effort to overcome the attendant frag-mentation of politics by bringing national attention to the plight of urban constituencies. It is worth pointing out, however, that neither in the 1930s nor the 1960s did the mayors willingly enter national politics on behalf of their constituencies. Rather, they were driven to do so by rising demands and escalating tumult in the cities. It remains to be seen whether, in the absence of comparable constituency mobilizations, mayors will take the initiative to try to restore the modest progress made earlier toward the nationalization—and democratization—of American politics.

CAN LOCAL POLICY AFFECT THE FLIGHT OF INDUSTRY FROM AMERICAN CITIES? A REVIEW OF LOCAL STRATEGIES TO COMBAT DEINDUSTRIALIZATION

BY LENA LUNDGREN GAVERAS AND WILLIAM JULIUS WILSON

BACKGROUND

The 1990 Urban Summit emphasized the importance of the city to our country's future prosperity. Among the important issues identified by Summit participants is the need to promote business and industrial investment in large urban areas. During the 1970s and early 1980s, many of the nation's larger cities struggled not only to attract new investments but simply to retain existing industries. Traditional industrial centers have experienced a massive movement of industrial plants out of the urban core. In the mid-1950s, the city of Chicago had over 10,000 manufacturing establishments that employed over 600,000 employees, including half a million blue-collar workers. By 1982, the number of plants had been cut in half, the number of overall jobs had been reduced to a mere 277,000, and the number of blue-collar workers had declined by 63 percent to fewer than 162,000. The problem is not unique to Chicago: cities such as New York, Philadelphia, Baltimore, and St. Louis have lost approximately half of their manufacturing jobs since the 1970s to the suburbs, the "Sunbelt," and foreign countries with cheaper labor.[1]

A shift from manufacturing to service industries and an explosion in the use of advanced technology affected employment opportunities in most large cities in the United States.[2] In many northern and northeastern cities, the increase in low-skill service industry jobs did not compensate for the loss of low-skill manufacturing jobs. For example, from 1970 to 1980, the number of jobs that did not require a high school degree in Chicago, Boston, Baltimore, and New York decreased between 40 and 60 percent, while the number of jobs requiring a minimum of a college degree increased between 47 and 77 percent.[3] However, even when the rise in white-collar service industries is accounted for, many northern and northeastern cities have had an overall employment decline.[4]

Urban economic restructuring has had a differential effect on employment rates and earnings across racial lines. While the real earnings of young, white, male high school dropouts declined by 17 percent between 1960 and 1980, the real earnings for their black counterparts plummeted by a staggering 47 percent.[5] Furthermore, the unemployment rate of twenty-year-old black men who were high school dropouts and who lived in the cities most highly affected by deindustrialization was more than twice that of a comparable group of black men who lived in the fastest-growing and least deindustrialized cities.[6] Cities that were the hardest hit by manufacturing losses also had the largest increase in black unemployment. While the nation's unemployment rate for blacks increased from 6.3 percent in 1970 to 12.3 percent in 1980, in Chicago it increased from 8.5 to 20.8 percent, in Detroit from 10 to 31 percent, and in Baltimore from 7 to 19 percent.[7]

Moreover, various studies indicate that large numbers of blue-collar workers end up unemployed for long periods after their place of employment shuts down. They also find that black males have longer jobless spells than white males. The decrease of stable, adequately paying jobs for young low-skill-level populations is connected to family breakdown and increases in crime and drug use in many larger cities.[8]

The disappearance of blue-collar jobs has also been linked to a growing concentration of poverty in the inner cities. New York City, Chicago, Philadelphia, Newark, and Detroit accounted for two-thirds of the 30 percent increase in ghetto poverty in the 1970s.[9] Compounding the problem of ghettoization, industrial plant closings result in a loss in tax revenue, while increasingly strapped city governments find themselves having to pay out a maximum level of unemployment compensation and welfare support.

The process of deindustrialization is too extensive to be countered solely by policies or strategies initiated by municipal authorities. Ira Katznelson has argued that "Urban authorities and citizens can hardly control the characteristics of the national economy, including the rate of its growth and the nature of the demand for labor, nor can they control characteristics of the industry in which an individual is employed such as profit rates, technology, unionization and the industry's relationship with government."[10] Issues of international trade and finance, which greatly affect decisions on where to locate production, need to be addressed both on a national and an international level.

Nonetheless, some of the problems leading to job losses in the manufacturing sector can be alleviated by local initiatives designed to halt or reverse the growing trend of plant shutdowns. These initiatives traditionally involved tax breaks or other forms of subsidy, but more innovative recent approaches focus on remedying poor management and ownership turnover, improving competitiveness, and protecting industrial land from residential real-estate development.

COMBATING THE EFFECTS OF DEINDUSTRIALIZATION: NEW LOCAL INITIATIVES

Local and state governments have made much use of economic subsidies to attract new industry. It has been estimated that during the 1980s, 50 percent of major new plant expansions and 90 percent of major new plant constructions benefited from at least one form of public investment: Urban Development Action Grants, Industrial Revenue Bonds, Job Training Partnership Act Funds, Community Development Block Grants, infrastructure improvements, property tax reductions or abatements, and various state funds for training and financing.[11]

Unfortunately, the use of the government subsidy strategy does not guarantee that a plant will either remain open for an extended period of time or increase the number of jobs available. For example, a recent study prepared for the comptroller of the city of Chicago found no increase in employment among the 95 industrial plants that received significant tax reductions ostensibly to increase employment.[12] Another study showed that of the 804 new jobs promised in 1988 by sixteen companies in Hammond, Indiana, that had received a tax abatement, only 75 had been created by 1990. Many large corporations are making transnational investment decisions these days, and from that perspective, urban communities in America seem less attractive as places for industrial investment.[13] Accordingly, many local governments and organizations are recognizing the need to create effective job-retention and job-creation strategies based on the strengths and resources available in the local community.

IDENTIFYING INDUSTRIES AT RISK

In 1988, the United States Congress passed the Worker Adjustment and Retraining Notification Act (WARN), requiring employers to provide a sixty-day notification of a plant shutdown under certain circumstances. However, many labor organizations, grass-roots organizations, and other groups involved in efforts to retain or renew the industrial base of cities argue that sixty days does not provide enough time to assess any alternatives to plant shutdowns or layoffs, such as identifying a new buyer or organizing a worker buy-out. In addition, training and jobs programs for dislocated workers need a longer time frame.

Accordingly, these groups advocate the creation of an early warning system in manufacturing plants to detect operational problems that may heighten the probability of plant closure and to alert workers and the general public. Conditions that increase the likelihood of a plant shutdown include ownership problems such as recent change in ownership, aging owners without designated successors, and ownership by an individual or corporation with a history of closing plants.[14] Management stability is also a good indicator: if a plant is facing imminent shutdown, the best managers are often transferred to other companies.

The Midwest Center for Labor Research (MCLR), a leading advocate of an early warning system, recommends the creation of an extensive network of representatives from labor, grass-roots organizations, and public officials, who would devise appropriate action to deal with the threat of plant shutdown. Early warning could help minimize community economic and social dislocations. The business community may perceive it as threatening or antagonistic, especially if the reason for a plant shutdown is management's decision to move a branch plant to another location. But in some instances, especially in the case of the small business community, the early warning system can be used in ways that are beneficial to business.

STRATEGIES TO PROMOTE LOCAL OWNERSHIP AS A RESPONSE TO PLANT SHUTDOWNS

The lack of succession in the ownership of a company is one of the more common reasons for a plant shutdown among smaller manufacturing plants. Recently, the state of Illinois funded an MCLR survey of all manufacturing companies in Chicago with fewer than 250 employees that had an owner age fifty- five and older. Of the 750 companies surveyed, approximately 52 percent had either no successor or a successor over the age of fifty-five.[15] These companies were defined as at risk for closing down. Since so many blue-collar employees work in the smaller manufacturing companies, this finding has important implications for understanding the increasing problems of economic dislocation in urban areas.[16]

If a local warning system is useful in identifying plants in danger of shutting down, so is knowledge of successful strategies to address the problem of successorship. New York State has created the nation's largest public agency, the Center for Employee Ownership and Participation (NYCEOP), to focus on economic development in the area of business succession. NYCEOP promotes worker ownership as its main strategy for nonfamily succession,[17] conducting workshops targeted to business owners on the suitability of worker ownership. The states of Ohio, Michigan, and Washington have similar programs that are either run through state or nonprofit agencies.

An effort generally regarded as one of the most successful in promoting worker ownership is that of the Naugatuck Valley Project in Western Connecticut. The Naugatuck Valley Project was developed in response to the problems of deindustrialization in the past decade. "Like those in similar areas elsewhere, the people of Naugatuck Valley have found that their established approaches have given them little leverage over deindustrialization. Conventional union tactics have exerted little influence over companies prepared to close up or sell the shop. Legislation to affect plant closing has been difficult to pass, and when passed has had limited effect."[18]

Established through the interest and involvement of more than fifty religious, labor, community, and small-business organizations, its aim is to allow the people of Naugatuck Valley to exert more influence over

their employment and economic base. The project has successfully organized several employee plant buy-outs. It has also aided the development
of new enterprises and was responsible for ensuring a link between urban
development in Naugatuck Valley and job preservation. Relying heavily on community organizing efforts, the project, states Jeremy Brecher,
"tries to mobilize concern about deindustrialization in unions, churches, and other organizations, and it tries to serve as a vehicle through which
those groups can bargain with corporations, government, and other powerful institutions."[19] Its primary strategies are to:

1) generate widespread support in the region for its programs;
2) create bargaining goals appropriate to each situation, with the understanding that employee ownership may not always be a feasible outcome;
3) promote local ownership to enhance employment stability; and
4) draw upon the resources of groups (accountants, lawyers, and
   business consultants) with special expertise in the business world.[20]

Another approach to deal with the problems of ownership succession
is provided by MCLR in Illinois. MCLR has developed a program to identify qualified minority buyers of companies in the Chicago region,
where a sizable percentage of the population is either black or Hispanic
but only 0.5 percent of the owners of manufacturing firms in the stan-
dard metropolitan statistical area (SMSA) are.[21]

MCLR argues that deindustrialization in Illinois has disproportionately
affected blacks and Hispanics for two major reasons: plant closings
occur much more frequently in older, inner-city sites than in newer
ones in the suburbs,[22] and layoffs frequently invoke the "seniority principle."[23] MCLR maintains that one way to deal with the problems of minority economic dislocation is to aid minority groups to "progress from being
victims of plant closings to partners" in job retention and expansion.[24]
Working with for-profit organizations, MCLR has been identifying and
training minority buyers for companies deemed suitable.[25]

PLANNED MANUFACTURING DISTRICTS

Conflict over land use inside the city limits is another cause of the loss
of manufacturing jobs in urban areas. In many cities, neighborhoods that
were industrial areas are being purchased by real estate developers in
order to create residential, office, or retail districts.[26] "Will the city's industrial culture withstand the forces of the global economy," asked Louis
Massoti, "only to be brought to its knees by a Yuppie culture that
would replace a $30,000-a-year steel job with $3.35 for packing groceries?"[27]

In response to this problem, some local governments are establishing
zoning devices, described as planned manufacturing districts (PMDs), to
protect industrial areas from use as residential and commercial sites. PMDs
are "intended to prevent factories and jobs from deserting the city as

property prices and taxes soar and affluent residential neighbors complain about truck and smoke pollution."[28] Neighborhood residents, businesses, and industries participate in a planning process to consider the needs and future of the neighborhood and to decide on geographic boundaries, use regulations, and special restrictions. In Chicago, following a campaign initiated by community organizations, an ordinance was passed in 1988 to establish PMDs. There is currently one PMD there, and plans have been made for two more. Other cities using or proposing to use a PMD strategy to protect manufacturing jobs are Baltimore, Boston, and Cleveland.

JOB-RETENTION AND JOB-CREATION STRATEGIES OF COMMUNITY ORGANIZATIONS

The role of small community organizations in local job-retention efforts is perhaps best exemplified by the Calumet Project—a coalition of twenty-two community organizations, unions, and churches—which operates in northwest Indiana[29] and the South Chicago Jobs Authority—a coalition of community organizations and unions located in heavily industrialized Gary, Indiana. The Calumet Project is involved not only in the development of an early warning system for plant shutdowns in East Chicago and northwest Indiana; it also provides research on the stability of local industries, builds coalitions among residents, unions, and businesses to work on strategies to prevent plants such as those with problems of ownership succession from shutting down, and actively monitors local industry's use of tax subsidies to curb tax abatement abuse.

The South Chicago Jobs Authority promotes the idea of using the skills of workers laid off by the steel mills to repair Chicago's declining infrastructure, with particular attention paid to the renovation of Chicago's bridge system. Many of the city's aging movable bridges have been identified as in need of either major repair or replacement.[30] The proposal by the South Chicago Jobs Authority could provide a model for the creation of meaningful jobs to alleviate the problems of economic dislocation created by deindustrialization.

CONCLUSION

The process of deindustrialization has increased economic dislocation in many urban neighborhoods. In the absence of effective national solutions, local governments have been compelled to identify strategies for retaining jobs and enhancing the employment base of the neighborhoods that have experienced the greatest job losses. A number of job-creation and job-retention efforts have been under way in several cities. It is too early to judge the success of any initiative, but future studies should be able to determine which local experiments are worthy of emulation nationwide.

Many of these strategies have originated on the grass-roots level through the efforts either of local community organizations or of workers affected by plant shutdowns. However, the number of people reached by these groups is small, and the services they provide are limited because of budgetary constraints and an orientation toward providing resources to a specific group, such as low-skilled or minority populations in a specific neighborhood.

It ought to be clearly recognized, that a large-scale effort to address the problems of deindustrialization can only be implemented on a national level. Problems such as the relocation of industries to countries abroad and the closing of branch plants whose central management has no tie to or interest in the community cannot be solved on a local level.

REFERENCES

Bluestone, Barry, Mary Huff Stevenson, and Chris Tilly. "The Deterioration in Labor Market Prospects for Young Men with Limited Schooling: Assessing the Impact of 'Demand Side' Factors." 1991. Draft, University of Boston.

Bound, John, and Harry J. Holzer. "Industrial Shifts, Skill Levels and the Labor Market for White and Black Males." Draft, Michigan State University, East Lansing, 1991.

Brecher, Jeremy. "If All the People Are Banded Together: The Naugatuck Valley Project." *Labor Research Review* 9, no. 2 (Fall 1986): 1–18.

Bureau of National Affairs. Daily Labor Reports (DLR). Washington D.C., July 7, 1988.

DuBois, Tom. "A Case for Increased Infrastructure Spending in Chicago and the Impact on the Demand for Steel." Draft, South Chicago Jobs Authority, 1989.

Eggers, Mitchell L., and Douglas S. Massey. "A Dynamic Analysis of Urban Poverty: Blacks in U.S. Metropolitan Areas Between 1970 and 1980." Population Research Center, NORC/University of Chicago, 1991.

Feekin, Lynn, and Bruce Nissen. "Early Warning of Plant Closing: Issues and Prospects." Unpublished draft, January 1991.

Goozner, Merrill. "Duluth Wins Plant Closing Case." *Chicago Tribune*, June 28, 1988.

Houston, Patrick. "When a City's Deal to Save Jobs Sours." *New York Times*, June 24, 1988.

Isidore, Chris. "Government Faulted for Lost Industries," *Post-Tribune* (East Chicago, Indiana), November 4, 1989.

Jargowsky, Paul A., and Mary Jo Bane. "Neighborhood Poverty: Basic Questions." In *Concentrated Urban Poverty in America*, ed. Michael T. McGeary and Lawrence E. Lynn, Jr. (Washington, D.C.: National Academy Press, 1990).

Kasarda, John D. "City Jobs and Residents on a Collision Course: The Urban Underclass Dilemma." Economic Development Quarterly 4, no. 4 (November 1990a): 313-19.

Kasarda, John D. "Structural Factors Affecting the Location and Timing of Urban Underclass Growth." *Urban Geography* 11, no. 3 (Summer 1990b): 234–64.

Katznelson, Ira. "The Crisis of the Capitalist City: Urban Politics and Social Control." In *Theoretical Perspectives on Urban Politics*, ed. Willis D. Hawley and Michael Lipsky (Englewood Cliffs, N.J.: Prentice-Hall, 1976), p. 229.

Kerson, Roger. "Planned Manufacturing Districts." Midwest Center for Labor Research, Chicago, 1990.

Kerson, Roger, and Greg LeRoy. "State and Local Initiatives in Development Subsidies and Plant Closings." Unpublished report, Federation for Industrial Retention and Renewal, Chicago, 1989.

LeRoy, Greg, Dan Swinney, and Elaine Carpentier. "Early Warning Manual against Plant Closings." Midwest Center for Labor Research, Chicago, 1988.

Lyons, Arthur, Spenser Staton, Greg Wass, and Mari Zurek. "Reducing Property Taxes to Promote Industrial Development: Does It Work? An Evaluation of Cook County's Industrial Incentive Real Estate Classifications." Center for Urban Affairs and Policy Research, Northwestern University, Evanston, Illinois, 1988.

Midwest Center for Labor Research. "The Deindustrialization of Chicago." A special report, Chicago, 1989a.

Midwest Center for Labor Research. "Intervening with Aging Owners to Save Industrial Jobs." A report to the Strategic Planning Committee of the Economic Development Commission Foundation of Chicago, 1989b.

Midwest Center for Labor Research. "Social Cost Analysis of Possible Shutdown of Brach Candy." Chicago, 1990.

Moss, Philip, and Chris Tilly. "Why Black Men Are Doing Worse in the Labor Market: A Review of Supply Side and Demand Explanations." Prepared for the Social Sciences Research Council Subcommittee on Joblessness and the Underclass, Massachusetts Institute of Technology, Cambridge, 1991.

Nissen, Bruce. "Union Battles against Plant Closings: Case Study Evidence and Policy Implications." Policy Studies Journal 18, no. 2 (Winter 1989–90): 382–95.

Podgursky, Michael, and Paul Swaim. "The Duration of Joblessness Following Plant Shutdowns and Job Displacement." University of Massachusetts, Amherst, 1987.

Ranney, David C. "Manufacturing Job Loss and Early Warning Indicators." Journal of Planning Literature 3, no. 1 (Summer 1988): 22–35.

Ranney, David C. "Transnational Production and Local Job Retention Strategies: A Research Proposal." Center for Urban Economic Development, University of Illinois, Chicago, 1990.

Schmidt, William E. "Chicago Plan Aims to Curb Factory Loss." *New York Times*, December 10, 1987, p. 1.

Wacquant, Loic J. D., and William Julius Wilson. "The Cost of Racial and Class Exclusion in the Inner City." *Annals of the American Academy of Political and Social Science* 501 (January 1989): 8–25.

Wilson, William Julius. *The Truly Disadvantaged: The Inner City, the Underclass, and Public Policy* (Chicago: University of Chicago Press, 1987).

Wilson, William Julius. "Public Policy Research and the Truly Disadvantaged." In The Urban Underclass, ed. Paul E. Peterson and Christopher Jencks (Washington, D.C., The Brookings Institution, 1991).

ENDNOTES

1. Kasarda, 1990a and 1990b, and Wacquant and Wilson, 1989, p. 13.

2. Ibid.

3. Ibid.

4. Kasarda, 1990a.

5. Bluestone, Stevenson, and Tilley, 1991.

6. Ibid.

7. Wacquant and Wilson, 1989.

8. Moss and Tilly, 1991.

9. Ghetto poverty refers to those among the poor who live in census tracts with poverty rates of at least 40 percent. See Wilson 1987.

10. Katznelson, 1976, p. 219.

11. Kerson and LeRoy, 1989.

12. Lyons, Staton, Wass, and Zurek, 1988. In recent years local governments have begun to enact legislation designed to make the business sector accountable for some of the public support received.

13. Ranney, 1990.

14. LeRoy, Swinney, and Carpentier, 1988.

15. Midwest Labor Research Center, 1989b.

16. Ibid.

17. Kerson and LeRoy, 1989.

18. Brecher, 1986, p. 1.

19. Ibid., p. 2.

20. Ibid.

21. Midwest Center for Labor Research, 1989b.

22. Ibid.

23. Ibid.

24. Midwest Center for Labor Research, 1989b.

25. Ibid. Unfortunately, MCLR's small size limits its ability to identify and train potential minority buyers and identify businesses in need of ownership.

26. Kerson, 1990.

27. Massoti, quoted in Schmidt, 1987.

28. Schmidt, 1987, p. 1.

29. Isidore, 1989.

30. DuBois, 1989.

THE REGIONAL CITY AND PUBLIC PARTNERSHIPS

BY H. V. SAVITCH, DANIEL SANDERS, AND DAVID COLLINS

CITY/SUBURBAN DISPARITIES

For decades the economic disparity between city and suburb has widened. The growing chasm is a major element in the intensification of the urban crisis. Much of the academic literature on cities dismisses central, or "core," cities as no longer the vital centers for their regions. Analysts have described central cores as "reservations for the poor,"[1] or "sandboxes" in which problems can be restricted,[2] or as "colonial" territories from which suburbanites can reap gains without paying costs.[3]

There may be a good deal of truth to some of these accounts: Ten years ago suburbs had per capita incomes that averaged 12 percent higher than their central cities. New data show that suburban incomes are now 68 percent higher. A decade ago 37 percent of those in poverty lived in central cities; today that figure is 43 percent.[4] After three decades of recitation, the litany on central city/suburban disparity is depressingly familiar, and future Census tallies are unlikely to give us cause for cheer.[5]

After reading the figures, the inference most readily drawn is that suburbs are growing at city expense.[6] The "bucket in the well" analogy is that suburbs draw affluent populations and investment capital from core cities, and if the city well is not completely dry, it is being emptied.

CITY/SUBURBAN INTERDEPENDENCE

Tempting as it may be, the image of a bucket in the well may be misleading. Cities and suburbs are interdependent; each shares (asymmetrically) in the fortunes of the other. Notwithstanding the continuing flow of residents to suburbs, many routinely return to central cities. A glance at transportation patterns in the United States shows that central cities remain the destination for 53 percent of all metropolitan trips.[7] Of those who have moved to suburbs, 20 percent still commute to central cities for their livelihoods.[8]

The future of cities and their suburbs may not be divergent but complementary. The seemingly inexorable flow of people to the suburbs may be a fact of American life, but the growth and prosperity of suburbs in a given metropolitan area may be an expression of the central city's vigor rather than its attenuation; indeed, troubled central cities often reflect low growth or economic weakness in their surrounding suburbs.

Scatterplots of the demographics of large, population-losing cities and their suburbs between 1980 and 1990 reveal the complementary nature of this relationship. Figure 1 relates population change in central cities to that of their respective suburbs.[9]

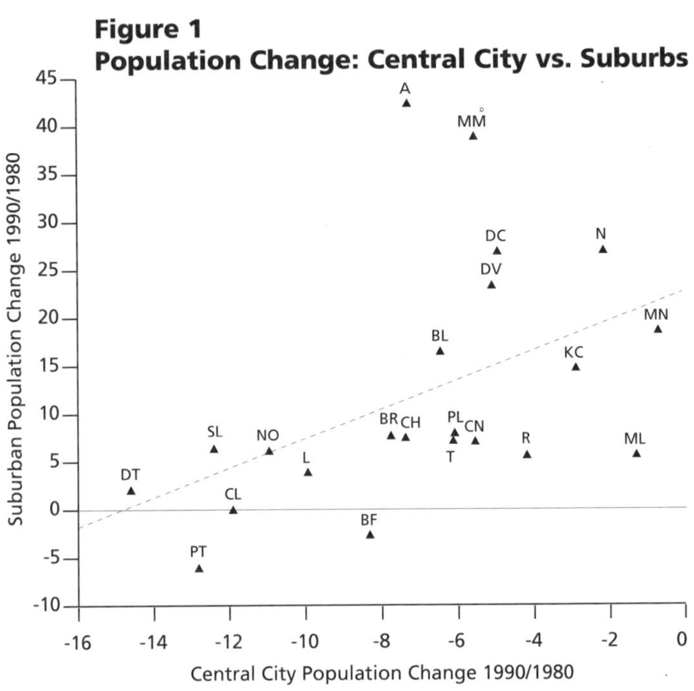

A	Atlanta	PT	Pittsburgh	MM	Memphis
DT	Detroit	BR	Birmingham	T	Toledo
NO	New Orleans	L	Louisville	CN	Cincinnati
BF	Buffalo	R	Rochester	MN	Minneapolis
DV	Denver	CH	Chicago	DC	Washington, D.C.
PL	Philadelphia	ML	Milwaukee	N	Norfolk
BL	Baltimore	SL	St. Louis		
KC	Kansas City	CL	Cleveland		

Cities in the upper right section of the figure (Norfolk, Memphis) have relatively low population loss in the urban cores and relatively high gains in their suburbs. Compare this with cities in the lower left side (Pittsburgh, Cleveland, Detroit, and Buffalo), which have experienced severe losses in their urban cores along with losses or only marginal gains in their suburbs.

The relationship between city and suburban population growth is so strong that the probability that this distribution could result by chance is only about one in forty. The slope of the regression line is upward, suggesting symbiosis—not downward, which would have suggested a parasitic relationship. The graph tells us that when central cities are hit by adversity (notably a declining industrial base), so too are their suburbs.

By itself, population decline or growth is not a sufficient indicator of how well localities are doing. There are occasions, for example, when prospering neighborhoods become less densely populated as they gentrify and residents demand more space. Any consideration of population must be linked not just to these raw numbers, but also to the characteristics of those who move and those who stay behind. Another way of looking at the relative strengths of cities and suburbs is to examine per capita income (pci). Figure 2 shows the pci discrepancy between cities and suburbs on the vertical axis. At the bottom of the vertical scale, city pci equals suburban pci, while toward the top suburbs more than double their city counterparts. The horizontal axis measures pci in dollars.

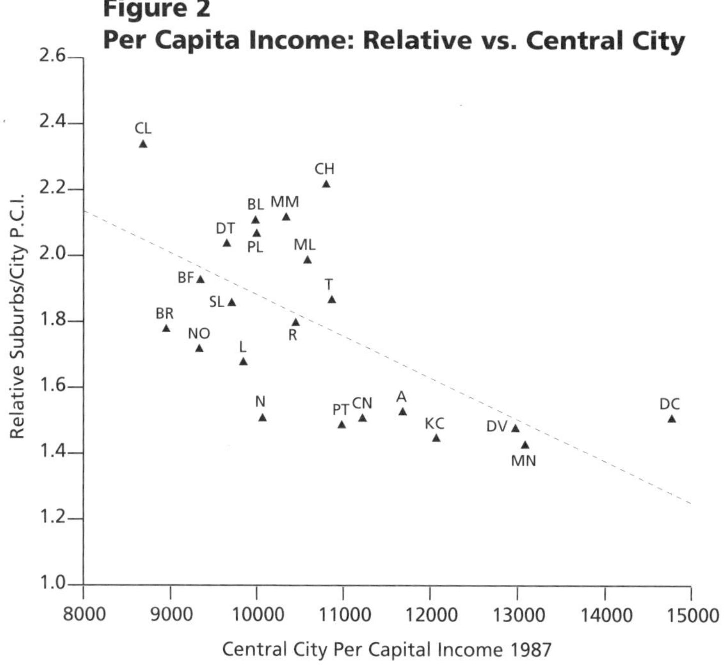

Figure 2
Per Capita Income: Relative vs. Central City

Note that where the income disparity between cities and suburbs is low, the cities are relatively prosperous. Thus, in Denver and Minneapolis, where suburban pci is only 40 percent above the urban cores, city residents still enjoy decent incomes. On the other hand, the suburbs of

Cleveland and Detroit have a pci double that of their urban cores, and residents of those cities have alarmingly low incomes. If it were the case that suburban income rises when the disparity with the central city is larger, we might entertain the common belief that suburbs simply drain central cities as their respective economies grow further apart. However, the opposite is true: central city pci and suburban pci tend to rise or fall together. Lower disparities between cities and suburbs go hand in hand with well-off metropolitan regions. As a whole, the metropolitan regions of Kansas City, Denver, Minneapolis, and Washington, D.C., are considerably better off than Detroit, Buffalo, and St. Louis. Healthier cities make for healthier metropolitan regions.

Tying per capita income to population change clarifies this link between city and suburb. Figure 3 shows city/suburban disparities on the horizontal axis compared to suburban population change on the vertical axis.

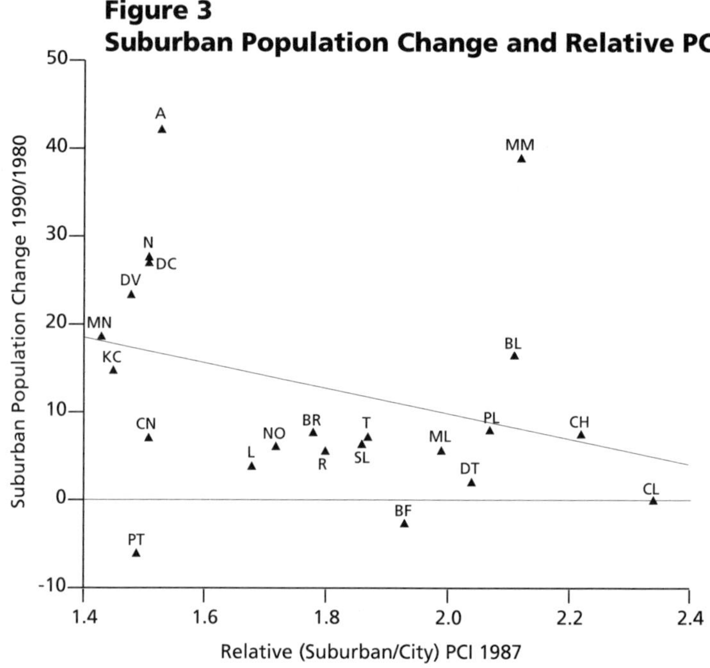

Figure 3
Suburban Population Change and Relative PCI

If flight from troubled cities really spurred surrounding suburbs, it would seem logical that both income disparities and suburban growth would rise together. In fact, income disparity and suburban population growth do not increase together; instead, one increases as the other declines.

Cities with growing suburbs, such as Atlanta, Norfolk, and Washington, D.C., have smaller income disparities than troubled cities with no suburban growth, such as Buffalo and Cleveland.

Although the chance of this pattern occurring because of random variation is one in four, the evidence shows a relationship between declining urban cores and suburban stagnation. The analogy of a bucket in the well is not as helpful as a recognition of interdependence.

BALANCING REGIONAL INTERESTS

What accounts for the mutuality of urban/suburban fortunes? One explanation is that moving to the suburbs does not afford a complete escape from city problems. Suburbanites continue to rely on the troubled central cities for work, or shopping, or entertainment, or special occasions. Those wishing to flee city problems may be more likely to choose healthy regions rather than settle for healthier suburbs.

Likewise, business firms either making start-up investments or considering relocation are inclined to move to a suburb in a healthy region rather than merely to a nearby suburb. Business investors are interested in a skilled work force, the long-term security of real estate values, the ease of transportation between localities, and other things that can often be found at a lower cost in healthy regions

Cities and suburbs both do well when they are part of regions that enjoy a balanced infrastructure. Industrial expansion depends upon the continued development of sewage and waste treatment facilities; commercial growth requires highways, airports, and decent mass transit; residential enhancement requires parks, recreational centers, and a clean environment. Metropolitan areas also do well when they enjoy balanced development between downtown centers and subregional centers. Vital downtowns can serve as hubs for office employment, professional services, retail outlets, governmental and legal institutions, culture, and, in general, functions that thrive upon sheer human agglomeration and daily contact. Subregional centers are often useful for light industry, back offices, small professional firms, local banking services, and shopping malls. This does not mean that functions are best parceled into neat categories without mix and diversification. However, certain businesses and pursuits may be more suitable for central cities, and others for outlying areas. All economic activity in a metropolitan area ought to be viewed as complementary, part of an organic whole.

In addition, prospering cities generate socioeconomic balance with their suburbs. Regions that are socially and economically integrated do better than segregated ones. Regions that have a corroding and menacing urban core do far worse.

The facts of this imbalance are borne out by data on suburban attitudes toward their core cities. In a survey of residents living outside 100 large cities, no less than 50 percent and up to 75 percent viewed the crises of their nearby cities as "serious" or "very serious." The threat of these problems was such that a substantial proportion of noncity residents (60 to 74 percent) were willing to pay more taxes in order to deal with them.[10] Is balance, then, the single critical factor in resolving the urban crisis? No, but revitalizing the central city can do a good deal toward achieving balance and improving a region's health. Cities and suburbs ought to plan for a commonly beneficial infrastructure. They ought to have the means to undertake the education of a common work force, capable of servicing downtowns as well as subregional centers. They ought to have the capacity to pool resources for better transportation and stronger service delivery. They ought to be prepared to enhance downtowns with "amenity districts" (which provide a higher level of services to business and residents as an inducement to locate in distressed urban cores).[11] Most important, they ought to be able to plan and attract development together, instead of tripping over each other in the competition for private investment.

PUBLIC PARTNERSHIPS

One way to enhance metropolitan regions is to develop public-to-public partnerships between local governments. The term "partnership" implies city-suburban cooperation, not compulsion. Cities and suburbs need to recognize ways in which their particular interests coincide so that public partnerships can benefit both.

Actually, localities have experimented, often successfully, with various forms of public partnerships by way of municipal consolidations, multitier government, regional councils, and ad hoc arrangements between localities. There is no single right way to bring about public partnerships—approaches depend upon the complex and varied conditions of cities, suburbs, and regions.

These differing approaches can be broken down into four basic patterns: (1) single-tier government (consolidation), which absorbs smaller units into an expanded, unified municipality; (2) two-tier (metropolitan) government, which retains the identity of smaller units but allows for the creation of a regional entity for specific purposes; (3) a loose confederation of governments that permits a common advisory council to coordinate or recommend common actions for a region; and (4) functional matrix governments (compacts), which allow for select services or resources to be merged or shared between different local governments.[12]

1. Consolidation entails the absorption of one or more localities into a single larger government. It is clean and comprehensive, but bringing about consolidation is politically difficult and risky for those who advocate it. Two examples of consolidation took place during the late 1960s

in Jacksonville and Indianapolis. The old city of Jacksonville plus four small municipalities and the former county of Duval were combined into a single municipality, with two differentiated service districts. Before consolidation Jacksonville faced serious outmigration, huge problems with the school system (financial insolvency, disaccredited schools), severe pollution (due to raw sewage and septic tanks), poor infrastructure (inadequate drainage, unpaved streets), and a soaring cost for municipal services.

After consolidation, property tax rates declined for both city and suburban taxpayers in nine of the first ten years.[13] Other taxes, however, increased because the new government expanded services and because of inflation. Following consolidation, $90 million was allocated to rebuild the sewer system, and 133 miles of new line were added. A new regional park was constructed, and recreational opportunities were expanded. Bond ratings improved, and fire insurance rates were lowered.[14] New countywide land-use planning, zoning, and building codes were passed. Though there is little hard evidence, new business investment was attributed to these improvements.[15]

In Indianapolis, sixty governmental units and special districts were replaced in 1969 by a single municipal-county system, called Unigov. Under Unigov, Indianapolis has a strong mayor/council system.

The city's property tax dropped after consolidation. In great part, the lowered rate was due to the city's enhanced ability to obtain federal and state aid. Indianapolis reportedly saved $84,000 annually in the early 1970s by centralizing purchasing. It also saved $360,000 in wages by reducing the number of sanitation trucks.[16] A major benefit was better management. Consolidation allowed the mayor to reorganize a number of smaller units into six departments. A comprehensive planning and development agency was created, and housing, parkland, and recreational facilities were expanded.

Unigov appears to have benefited the central business district. By 1973 the volume of downtown construction had increased fourfold.[17] Urban renewal projects have also been boosted by using a citywide tax, specifically designated for this purpose. Although unpopular with suburbanites, this funding combined with federal funding to benefit neglected portions of the inner city.[18]

2. Two-tier (metropolitan) government creates a division of labor between a regional government, which handles problems best suited to "wide" governmental control (air pollution, waste treatment), and local governments, which manage functions best suited to "narrow" supervision (parking regulations). Two-tier government allows for accommodation between governments but also has been known to encourage friction between localities. Some examples of two-tier government are in Nashville-Davidson County (Metro Nashville) and Miami-Dade County (Metro Dade).

Metro Nashville operates under a mayor/council form of government. A mayor, vice mayor, and county council are elected to four-year terms. Under state law, Metro Nashville has all the powers of both a municipality and of a county and (like Jacksonville) provides services within two differentiated districts. What makes Metro Nashville a two-tier system is that six municipalities retain separate status, so that residents within these areas enjoy a combination of their own services plus those they may acquire from the metropolitan tier.

Before Metro, the county intended to release sewage into the Cumberland River. After Metro came into being, sewage facilities for the county were extended and tied into a common system. The Nashville Thermal Transfer plant, which generates steam from burning solid waste, has reduced energy and landfill costs. Two-tier government also allowed police and fire services to be reorganized and provided with enhanced training. Health, hospital, and welfare programs were enlarged, and improvements were made to the library, school, and park system.

In Miami, a home rule charter amendment was adopted, giving Dade County commissioners power to assume many of the functions of twenty-six municipalities, but still leaving those municipalities intact. A county mayor is elected at-large and presides over the nine-member commission. Metro Dade has been hampered by its inability to carry out comprehensive land-use planning and zoning, which are still left with member cities. Because of these limitations, Metro Dade achievements were relegated to advantages of scale, largely brought about by reorganizing services (police, parks, housing code enforcement) or by taking over some important facilities, such as the seaport.[19]

3. A loose confederation, or metropolitan council, brings together a number of localities under a common political umbrella. Such councils are usually advisory. Their cooperative features make them politically attractive, but reliance on consensus weakens their ability to carry out policy.

In Minneapolis-St. Paul, the state legislature created a seventeen-member council to oversee seven counties within the Minneapolis region. The council is appointed by the governor and confirmed by the Senate. Its primary responsibility consists of drawing up a Comprehensive Development Guide for the region to ensure orderly growth. The council also promotes efficient use of facilities, coordinates policies, and develops flexible policy standards. It reviews land-use plans by local governments and oversees and coordinates special service districts.

The metropolitan council is not a general-purpose regional government, nor is it a voluntary council of governments. It does not provide services or zone land. Instead, it serves as a coordinating council that focuses its energies on policy considerations, conducts planning studies, and makes recommendations for the region. Since its inception, the council has established a regional planning process and undertaken general functions regarding the zoo, regional parks, sewers, and solid waste. To date, its most impressive achievement has been to establish a "fairshare" housing plan, under which individual localities agree to accept a percentage of housing for low- and moderate-income families.

4. Functional matrix governments (compacts) are arrangements, sometimes temporary, allowing localities to selectively cooperate with one another over specific objectives. They are flexible and can be used to resolve limited problems but are often incomplete in scope. Two compacts that are quite different from one another are Louisville-Jefferson County and the Port Authority of New York and New Jersey.

The Louisville metropolitan area is ribboned by about one hundred local governments, struggling to hold down taxes, enhance services, and attract industry. In 1986, the central city concluded a twelve-year agreement with Jefferson County to share in tax revenues, set up joint efforts at economic development, and divide responsibilities for maintaining certain services (air pollution, health, planning).

Thus far, the results have been satisfying. City and county have been able to improve their crime-fighting apparatus through such innovations as a joint task force on narcotics. The issuance of licenses and permits is more efficient, and the costs of running some agencies are reduced.

The compact has also made it somewhat easier for both governments to undertake an airport expansion and the enlargement of the region's urban enterprise zone.[20] While competition for economic development exists, it has been less intense because of the compact's provision for tax sharing. Over the last five years the compact has allowed for the redistribution to the city of $4.3 million in tax revenues.

The Port Authority of New York and New Jersey is well-known. Established in 1921 and run by a bistate board and a chief executive, the Authority has been at the forefront of the region's economic development. It manages some twenty-five facilities—from airports to bridges, tunnels, bus terminals, and a commuter rail system. It has also built some of New York's best-known skyscrapers: the twin towers of the World Trade Center. The Authority has a reputation for being self-protective and hard-boiled, but it is hard to imagine the region's vibrancy and magnitude without the Port Authority.

PUTTING PUBLIC PARTNERSHIPS TO WORK

Structure shapes behavior, and it can be used to shape stronger metropolitan regions for both cities and suburbs. Metropolitan areas are fragmented into bits and pieces, but public partnerships can knit the pieces together. What kinds of partnerships are most feasible for cities and suburbs must vary according to conditions and preferences of localities. But there are roles the federal government, the states, and localities can play in encouraging those partnerships. For starters, we suggest the following:

—The federal government should adopt a Public Partnership Act designed to promote partnerships between local governments and pay for start-up costs. As a first step, federal support should be used to defray the costs of planning, staffing, and implementing these partnerships. *—The Public Partnership Act should provide long-range funding tied to achievable and measurable objectives.* The idea is to sustain public partnership innovations that work and have a continuous track record of achievement. Thus, public partnerships designed to achieve educational excellence can be evaluated by measures of scholastic performance over a period of time, and grants can be awarded on a cumulative basis. Similar grants can be established for local partnerships that undertake capital expenditures for waste treatment, for environmental enhancement (clean air, green space), or for rebuilding infrastructure (sewage, mass transit).

—The states should be relied upon to identify, orchestrate, and support public partnerships. States have played an active role in consolidating local governments, in establishing metropolitan councils, and in approving multitier governments. States pass on to local governments the right to annex land or join in compacts. States are best able to identify what kinds of partnerships are best suited for different communities and ought to establish local offices for encouraging partnerships.

—Various types of public partnerships should not be viewed as distinct, but as part of a continuum in which one type of partnership makes the other possible. Regions should build upon stages of the process that have proved themselves. Thus, localities might use compacts for a period of time and, assuming success, decide at a later date to adopt two-tier government.

—Federal, state, and regional authorities should recognize center-city downtowns as commercial hubs that can be linked to regional subcenters. Public partnerships should be used to promote and support "amenity zones" in downtown centers as well as regional subcenters. These zones can furnish enhanced services, such as additional cleaning, lighting, and security, as well as capital investments for street furniture and light rail transit.

In the final analysis, central cities are not expendable; they are vital parts of their metropolitan areas. The evidence of regional independence indicates that in the long term, suburban interests will benefit by helping central cities deal with their problems. The appropriate metaphor for a healthy regional city is that of a full well from which many buckets can draw.

REFERENCES

Advisory Commission on Intergovernmental Relations. *Substate Regionalism and the Federal System, vol. 2: Case Studies* (Washington, D.C.: Government Printing Office, 1973).

Alcaly, R. E., and D. Mermelstein, eds. *The Fiscal Crisis of American Cities* (New York: Vintage Books, 1977).

Chinitz, B., ed. *City and Suburb: The Economics of Metropolitan Growth* (Englewood Cliffs, N.J.: Prentice-Hall, 1964).

City University of New York. *Americans and Their Cities*. A survey report to The Urban Summit, prepared by the C.U.N.Y. Office of Urban Affairs in conjunction with the Robert Wagner, Sr. Institute and Schulman, Ronca & Bucuvalas, Inc., 1990.

Ledebur, L. C. *City Fiscal Distress: Structural, Demographic and Institutional Causes*. A research report from the National League of Cities, Washington, D.C., 1991.

Long, N. E. "The City as Reservation." *The Public Interest*, no. 25 (Fall 1971): 22-38.

Nathan, R. P., and C. Adams. "Understanding Central City Hardship." *Political Science Quarterly* 91, no. 1 (Spring 1976): 47–62.

Orski, K. *New York Times*, March 13, 1982, p. 25.

Pisarski, A. E. *Commuting in America* (Westport, Conn.: Eno Foundation for Transportation, 1987).

Research Atlanta. *The Urban Consolidation Experience in the United States* (Atlanta: Research Atlanta Inc., 1987).

Savitch, H. V. "Black Cities/White Suburbs: Domestic Colonialism as an Interpretive Idea." *Annals of the American Academy of Political and Social Science* 439 (September 1978): 118-34.

Savitch, H. V. "Boom and Bust in the New York Region: Implications for Government Policy." In *Economic Prospects for the Northeast*, ed. H. W. Richardson and J. H. Turek (Philadelphia: Temple University Press, 1985).

Stanback, T. M., Jr., and R. V. Knight. *Suburbanization and the City* (Montclair, N.J.: Allanheld, Osmun & Co., 1976).

Sternlieb, G. "The City as Sandbox." *The Public Interest*, no. 25 (Fall 1971): 14-21.

Stowers, G., and R. K. Vogel. "Miami." In *Big City Politics*, ed. H. V. Savitch and J. C. Thomas (Newbury Park, Calif.: Sage Publications, 1991).

Tabb, W. K., and L. Sawers. *Marxism and the Metropolis* (New York: Oxford University Press, 1984).

ENDNOTES

1. Long, 1971.

2. Sternlieb, 1971.

3. Savitch, 1978.

4. Ledebur, 1991.

5. Nathan and Adams, 1976.

6. Chinitz, 1964; Alcaly and Mermelstein, 1977; Stanback and Knight, 1976; Tabb and Sawers, 1984.

7. Pisarski, 1987.

8. Ibid.

9. We include in our sample only those metropolitan areas in which the central city had a 1980 population of 200,000 or more. We restricted our sample to population-losing cities for two reasons. One is that some population-gaining cities have annexed suburbs during the decade, making it impossible to draw valid comparisons. The second, and more important, reason is that it is among the population-losing cities that we might expect to see suburbs benefiting at the expense of their central cities. Thus, we framed the question in a manner that strengthens the case of the thesis we have come to reject. Further, we should note that one population-losing city was excluded: Newark, whose statistics are distorted by the manner in which the Census Bureau counts Bloomfield, Plainfield, and Montclair as suburbs of Newark rather than New York City. Finally, we should note that for purposes of consistency and comparability, we have relied on the same group of twenty-two cities and suburbs in subsequent tables (only one of these had a 1990 metropolitan population of fewer than 800,000).

10. City University of New York, 1990.

11. Orski, 1982; Savitch, 1985.

12. The four patterns are heuristic typologies best utilized for classification and analysis. In reality, some of the examples cited under these patterns mix different features.

13. Research Atlanta, 1987, p. 34.

14. Ibid., p. 50.

15. Ibid., passim.

16. Ibid.

17. Ibid., p. 61.

18. There is a great deal of debate on the alleged benefits of consol-

idated government. Studies do show variation in tax consequences and savings for local government. Thus, some types of governments may find consolidation to be more costly (partly because it generates a greater demand for more services). On balance, however, studies show less per capita expenditure and greater citizen satisfaction after consolidation. See Research Atlanta, 1987.

19. Advisory Commission on Intergovernmental Relations, 1973; Stowers & Vogel, 1991.

20. Neither the enterprise zone nor airport expansion is without its critics. For particulars on the enterprise zone, see the *New York Times*, October 31, 1990.

URBAN AID AND THE "EXPENSIVE PEOPLE"

BY RICHARD P. NATHAN

During the Urban Summit conference held in New York City November 11–13, 1990, Stephen Frazier interviewed two of the mayors who attended, David Dinkins of New York and Federico Peña of Denver, on the NBC "Today" show. He asked them: "How do you help the expensive people?" The word "expensive people" sticks in my mind. It says a lot about the current social condition of the United States. The concentration of social problems in blighted urban neighborhoods is, I believe, a new experience for this country. The word "underclass" is widely used to describe those affected by the problems of danger, drugs, deviance, and dependency in the most distressed urban zones.

My social science friends resist using the word "underclass," claiming it is stigmatizing and politically unwise. In my view, this argument about semantics is pointless. The genie is out of the bottle; it doesn't matter what terms social scientists choose. The phrase has stuck, and it is widely used in the media to signify a condition that involves the common values and behavior of people who live in particular kinds of urban areas.

In this essay for the Urban Summit, I concentrate not on the diagnostic side of the equation, but rather on solutions—specifically on the ways and amount by which urban aid could be provided to deal more effectively with the concentration of "expensive people" in cities.

From a tactical point of view, I believe it is better to concentrate on people rather than on places in considering urban aid, even though space is a key characteristic of the new problems we face. Concentrating on people avoids isolating large cities and particular groups in political process. It is true that the most severe urban problems are concentrated in large, older cities that have lost industry and population in recent periods. But the same problems can be found in newer cities, small cities, and in suburban neighborhoods that closely resemble the most distressed inner-city areas in their social and economic characteristics.

Lyndon Johnson could mount his Great Society in the 1960s on a broad basis to heal the sick, care for the aged, aid minorities through civil rights protections and equal opportunity programs, and educate children in better ways. A generation later, the social policy landscape has changed, and the political landscape has changed as well. Victims of AIDS, the homeless, crack addicts, violent members of youth gangs, all are caught in a culture of deviance in the inner city and in other troubled neighborhoods.

They lack jobs and economic opportunities. They have weak constituencies, and their needs have a narrow political appeal to the general public.

I use the phrase "culture of deviance" in referring to these concentrated issues of urban distress because I am impressed by the growing consensus among experts on urban conditions that the most severe problems we face today involve more than economics. They involve attitudes and behavior that are environmentally reinforced and that drag people down—that is, keep them from adhering to widely shared societal norms.

In the worst inner-city areas, because of peer pressure, many youths are reacting as if it is deviant behavior to "say no" to drugs, stay in school, get a regular job and keep it, and support one's children, family, and community. Of course, similar behavior is also found in better-off neighborhoods, but it is much more prevalent in long-deteriorating pockets of urban poverty such as Bushwick in Brooklyn, the West Side of Chicago, or Miami's Liberty City.

However much social deviance contributes to the problems of the inner city, programs to attack these problems cost money. And here, unfortunately although it is broadly held in public finance theory that cities cannot go it alone, that they cannot by themselves solve the social problems within their borders, that overlying governments—state and national—bear a responsibility for the redistribution of resources to deal with social needs, in practice things have not worked out well for cities. The national government pulled back in the 1980s from the social agenda. And the states, although their spending rose in the 1980s, now face serious fiscal pressures and are retrenching.

At the Urban Summit, the assembled mayors engaged in a wide-ranging substantive and political discussion of what can be done. As a first premise, they agreed that an effective program cannot be a program to save New York, big cities, or the underclass. Intellectually, such a direct approach focused on burden sharing to assist the largest and most troubled cities makes good sense and appeals to any of the people who care most about meeting urban needs. On sheer efficiency grounds, there is a strong case for a highly targeted aid program. Nevertheless, it is to the credit of the mayors who attended the Urban Summit that they agreed that the themes and aims of new urban initiatives must be broad and positive. Broad in the sense that they must encompass the interests of many groups concerned about better ways to meet domestic policy needs. Positive in the sense that the case for new domestic programs should not just lament the problems of the urban poor, but should also highlight the constructive nature of new social spending.

FIVE THEMES

A central question is, How can we craft a broad and positive package of increased federal aid to meet domestic needs that can win enactment in the country and in Congress? I suggest five themes:

1. **Children.** As a society, we should have compassion for children. The evidence suggests that saving children at an early age is more efficient than trying to intervene later on. In a subtle way, such an emphasis involves a triage policy, reaching in to save people (children and families) where the prospects for success are greatest and the benefits most long term.

2. **Competitiveness.** It is vital to our economic well-being in an increasingly competitive world to upgrade the nation's labor force. Our working-age population is diminishing. It is estimated that in the first decade of the next century the number of persons age 25–44 will decline by 15 percent. At the same time, our education system is seriously deficient in imparting basic skills to new entrants and immigrants and to people already in the work force. We need to improve the capacity of our schools to save children caught in cycles of despair and distress in the inner city and to strengthen job training and remediation programs to upgrade the skills of people already in the work force.

3. **Washington must act.** We should challenge the decision made by the federal government in 1990 to freeze national priority setting in the budget agreement. Policymakers inside the Beltway apparently got tired of making tough decisions. They called a moratorium, putting the federal government on automatic pilot for at least three years, and maybe more like five. This is not the American way of governing.

4. **Institution building.** A critical aim of any new domestic federal aid program must be to focus on what works. It must strengthen the management capacity of states, localities, and nonprofit groups to turn good policy intentions into good results for people. Implementation is the neglected frontier of American government. It is wrong to allow high government officials in Washington to get away with high-sounding discussions of new "empowerment" strategies as a substitute for real-money programs that bolster the institutions that deal with our most important social needs.

5. **Targeting.** The fifth theme is important but has to be treated carefully. Targeting federal grant-in-aid funds on distressed communities is good social policy and good economics. It can appeal to conservative groups as well as liberals. It makes sense to concentrate public spending on the places that have the deepest and most serious needs. Other countries do a better job than we do in targeting their domestic programs. Such targeted policies, if carefully crafted, can be made a selling point of a new federal aid program to meet social needs.

GUIDELINES

Next, we need to ask, what guidelines should be used to select the programs to include in a package of increased domestic federal aid. I suggest four guidelines:

1. The programs should be big enough to make a difference and not just demonstration programs.

2. They should be reasonably familiar, in many cases expanding or building on existing programs that have stood the test of time and have good redistributive properties.

3. They should be relatively simple to describe.

4. They should give emphasis to the point made above about improving management and program implementation.

"CARE AND SHARE" PROGRAM

I turn now to specific programs. ***I recommend a 5-year program that would shift considerable funds, say, up to $5 billion compounded each year, or $75 billion in total, from other budgetary areas to the domestic sector.***

In the first year of the program, there could be three elements in the package, beginning with the expansion of what is presently the most flexible urban aid program and has survived the test of time from the Nixon "New Federalism" period, the Community Development Block Grant program. This block grant is a close cousin to the revenue-sharing program, which was inaugurated under Nixon in 1972 at $5 billion per year in flexible grant funding to states and localities. (Revenue sharing ended in 1986 under President Reagan, after providing $85 billion to states and cities in its fourteen-year lifetime.) The Community Development Block Grant now provides $3 billion per year, concentrated on cities of more than 50,000 in population and large urban counties. The targeting of this program could be improved, but it is a good program and should be expanded.

As a second component of this new strategy, another federal aid program that has stood the test of time is the "Chapter 1" grants for elementary and secondary education, focusing on children from poor families. Chapter 1 is currently operating at $5 billion, and also should be expanded.

Third, I suggest the creation of "Children's Action Grants" to be used by state governments to improve the management of and to coordinate children's services in distressed areas. Governor Mario Cuomo is doing this in New York under his "Neighborhood Based Initiative." This gets state government into the picture. It focuses on children and institution building. I see particular promise in aid to family and children's neighborhood centers—like settlement houses of an earlier day. These institutions, both in the poorest urban neighborhoods and newly emerging working-class minority and immigrant neighborhoods, can be a strong force for social change.

As these programs gain acceptance, a drive needs to be made to establish minimum national welfare payment level for families, combined with welfare fiscal relief to the states. I favor incremental steps for welfare reform as a component of a larger social investment program in the second and third years of the plan. Other elements that could be added in subsequent years are more spending for Head Start and children's health care, including prenatal care and immunization; expanded welfare work and training initiatives; and expansion of the "Children's Action Grant" program for the states. A development bank for infrastructure was included in President Jimmy Carter's National Urban Program in 1978 but was never realized. Such an institution could be revived as part of this new urban-aid package.

Of course, advocates of increased social spending cannot duck the question of where the money should come from. In the long run, it is my view that we should shift money to the domestic area by downsizing the mission and manning of the defense establishment and the space program. Beyond that, if necessary, a tax increase, perhaps a consumption tax combined with investment tax incentives, should be considered.

THE WASHINGTON POLICY GAME

Think of this as the Washington policy game. For that is what it is. Any number can play. Good players are smart about the details. Using themes, guidelines, and examples like the five-year plan sketched above, there are many variations of substance, politics, numbers, phasing, and programs. But the net result is what counts: ***To form a successful coalition to win popular and political support for new federal aid to meet urgent domestic needs.***

Domestic policy initiatives take basically two forms—comprehensive and incremental. The term "comprehensive" refers to large, bold schemes to sort out functions and reform American government. The second type of strategy, "incremental," refers to step-by-step, lower-visibility initiatives along the lines proposed above. There is no one right approach for all seasons. But in American domestic policy, windows of opportunity for comprehensive domestic policies are few and far between. Given the budget battles we face at this time, there should be a strong preference for the lower-profile, incremental approach. I submit that the is approach is historically and quantitatively the main route to progress in U.S. domestic policy affairs.

THE MANAGEMENT CHALLENGE

Earlier, I referred to institution building as the neglected frontier of domestic policy. I urged that it be highlighted in any new domestic program. When we put up a flag for a new program, we need to ask, "Will the troops salute, will they march? Will the intended changes in the way government bureaucracies behave be translated into good results for people and communities?" Implementation is a critical dimension of U.S. domestic policy.

There are no magic formulas to improve management in government. A key requirement is to have our top officials be men and women who devote time and energy and have the leverage to be change agents to make sure that new policies penetrate public bureaucracies. We need to give these leaders more help through such measures as relaxing civil service procedures and other management constraints that have been overbuilt into American government. We also need to recognize that ours, like it or not, is a federal system of divided sovereignty. States have major roles to play in improving the management of domestic programs.

ROLE OF THE STATES

Students of urban and social policy must understand the federalism dimension of urban policy. Unfortunately, there is a great deal of ignorance about the structure and roles of American governments, much of it found in Washington. States play the crucial middleman role in social policy. My colleague Steven Gold has presented a useful five-point summary of advice for states in meeting urban needs:

1. Have the state take over financial responsibility for city museums, libraries, zoos, and other cultural activities that serve many people who are not city residents.

2. Have the state take over or provide substantial aid for hospitals that primarily serve the poor, local universities and community colleges, courts, and welfare programs.

3. Set up regional bodies with responsibility for transit, housing, and other functions that are financially burdensome (including area-wide activities such as museums that are not taken over by the state, in line with the previous option).

4. Create a tax base-sharing program such as the one in the Twin Cities to even out benefits of new investments that tend to accrue disproportionately to certain cities.

5. Revise aid distribution formulas to target more assistance to central cities, for example, by placing greater weight on "need" in revenue sharing or by cushioning the effect of declining enrollment in school aid formulas.*

---

* Steven Gold, *Reforming State-Local Relations: A Practical Guide* (Denver: National Council of State Legislatures, 1989), p. 151.

City governments do not have a big role in financing social programs, although there are some prominent exceptions. The most prominent exception is New York City, where the Urban Summit was held. New York is a combined city and county with its own city-operated hospitals and school district, and because of the way the state government operates, the city pays a large share of welfare spending. Most municipalities in America are not like this. The main responsibilities of most city governments are public safety (police and fire), some capital spending (streets, sewers, and so forth), and housekeeping functions.

States rule the roost when it comes to responsibility for the policies, finances, and management of social services. The U.S. federal government has few direct domestic programs, and has been cutting back on its grant-in-aid role for over a decade, increasingly doing more of its domestic policy business through mandates rather than money.

▲　　　▲　　　▲

Many of the mayors at the Urban Summit observed that a critical challenge of urban policy leadership in the current period is the mobilization of organizations and interests to capture the attention of the media in a way that will convince the public that it is both in our economic interest and morally right to increase the federal government's commitment to the domestic public sector. The summit conference was held before the Persian Gulf War broke out, when there was an expectation that the end of the cold war would produce a "peace dividend" for the cities. We can only hope that there soon will be an opening for such a peace dividend. The case for action is compelling. The increased federal aid program outlined in this paper is modest in relation to the size of the challenge.

Big-City Mayors and the News Media:
Changing the Image of Cities

BY MARGARET T. GORDON

Although members of the press were barred from attending the working sessions of the mayors' Urban Summit, the journalists were present every minute in the minds of the mayors and their aides. It could reasonably be argued the news media were the dominant influence at the Summit. The rules of participation, the language and symbols the mayors developed, the order in which the issues were presented, the "packaging," and ultimately the issues themselves were shaped by how the mayors and their aides thought their "urban compact," later titled *In the National Interest*, would play with the reporters waiting outside the closed conference room doors. The mayors were certain that how the journalists characterized the final document would significantly affect the attitudes of President Bush and the U.S. Congress toward cities. If the media portrayed the mayors' message as the same old story—holding out their collective tin cup for more federal aid—the mayors predicted little response. If, however, the media interpreted the Summit document as the unanimously adopted statement of powerful leaders of 100–120 million[1] Americans living in cities which, "like a mighty engine," were "pulling all of America into the future,"[2] and if they reported that strong cities were "in the national interest," then the mayors thought they would be not only heard, but heeded, in Washington.

During the two-day meeting, many of the mayors came to realize that they themselves had helped foster the prevailing view of cities as scary places full of problems solvable only by massive infusions of federal aid. They decided to reshape their own perceptions and those of others into images that stressed the positive contributions of urban areas to American culture, education, industry, communication, and finance. In the process, they would transform their image from that of tin-cup beggars of federal donations to those of drivers of "mighty engines," pulling hard in the national interest. They devised a media strategy that would seek first to alter the perceptions of journalists about cities, and through the journalists, the views of federal politicians and the public. The mayors knew this would not be an easy task.

Since they were successful politicians from cities with populations of over 200,000 that support daily and weekly newspapers and several broadcast outlets, all of the mayors attending the Summit had considerable experience with the media. Some mayors, of course, had more media experience than others because they had held elective office longer, because they presided in larger media markets, and/or because their administrations had received more media attention. Whether they were good at it or not, whether they enjoyed it or not, most mayors[3] regard having to deal with the media as a necessary fact of life in the 1990s. Whatever their individual experiences, all the mayors believed it was wise to craft a media strategy rather than leave their relationships with the journalists attending the Summit to chance. Their combined practical wisdom encouraged them to begin to grapple with ways of combating negative images of cities early in the Summit. They would seek fresh angles[4] to entice journalists, potential headlines, and anecdotes that could be turned into good[5] media stories.

The mayors believed there was a largely untold—and certainly not generally understood—good story about the way in which federal responsibilities had devolved during the Reagan years to the states and then to the cities, without any increases (in fact, with decreases) in resources to deal with the problems. At the same time, the mayors believed they had to come up with a new angle, a new way to frame the issues, in order to get the New York media, and perhaps their hometown media, to feature the revised image they wanted to promote. Their pre-Summit draft document, entitled "The Urban Compact," suggested a united, determined group of mayors whose unanimity could be politically threatening. Ultimately, they chose a more complicated image of cities as "mighty engines pulling all of America into the future in the national interest."

This paper describes the process by which the mayors arrived at their strategy and presents observations about the news media, urban problems, and public policy.

BEFORE THE SUMMIT

Six to eight weeks before the Summit was to take place, Bill Lynch, deputy mayor of New York City, asked Sandy Silverman of M. Booth and Associates, a New York public relations firm, to prepare a plan for press strategy and logistics.[6] Given the decision to bar the press from the key sessions, the committee wanted Silverman to help determine how it could maximize positive[7] coverage both in New York and in other mayors' hometowns.

Silverman designed a press plan and outlined it in two advance letters to the press secretaries of all the participating mayors. "Like a Mighty Engine, Urban America Pulls All of America into the Future" was to be proclaimed on banners at opening and closing press conferences, in meeting rooms, and on notebooks and podiums throughout the Sunday to Tuesday meeting. Her letters informed the mayors and their aides there would be a thirty-minute briefing "covering the major points" for the mayors before an opening press conference on Sunday afternoon (generally a slow news time and therefore more likely to be attended by journalists). The Summit would be handled as a breaking news event, with notices of the press conference to local and national media on the daybooks[8] of the news and specialized wires. The Sunday press conference was scheduled for a small room, "to better give a sense of immediacy and crowding," said Silverman. Although Mayor Dinkins would open the press conference by reading a prepared statement, Silverman advised against too much orchestration because it "kills spontaneity." There was to be a closing press conference Tuesday noon, at which the mayors would present the finished urban compact.

AT THE SUMMIT

Opening Press Conference. In his opening statement at the Sunday press conference, Mayor Dinkins said that the mayors had taken the extraordinary step of convening, because the extraordinary challenges faced by cities required extraordinary measures. Dinkins said he had invited them to New York "to begin a new era of cooperative, strategic planning, and not a moment too soon." He said that ten years ago federal sources constituted 19.4 percent of New York City's budget but that the federal share had been cut back to 9.7 percent. He promised, "The Urban Summit will put cities back into the federal debate—and our Urban Compact, which will be drafted on Tuesday—will provide a national urban agenda to reshape our cities and society." He noted that together the mayors represented well over 100 million people and a very substantial number of voters. Dinkins's remarks highlighted the old image of poor cities ignored by the federal government and indicated that the mayors, united, planned to change things.

Mayor Flynn of Boston, soon to be head of the U.S. Conference of Mayors, was the first to tell the fifty to sixty journalists in attendance that the "tin cup" approach was passé, and that the Urban Summit would signal a new approach. "We must point out how important cities are to the economic health of the nation. It's the cities that have the problems, but also we are the economic engines that drive the nation. We want to be dealt with seriously, and we are dealing from strength," said Flynn. In turn, other mayors showed support and enthusiasm for the Summit and indicated some of their own priorities—improving urban education, eliminating drug-related crimes, passing gun control legislation, and creating jobs for the unemployed.

The first question from a reporter was a reflection of an old image: "Where will the money come from to solve the problems of the cities?" Mayor Dinkins responded that New York gets back only 77 percent of each dollar it pays in taxes.

This and other questions allowed the mayors to discuss a range of issues reflecting both old and new perceptions—from the war on drugs and the need for gun control to the need for a variety of public/private and public/public (e.g., city-county) partnerships and "report cards" assessing elected officials.

The Working Sessions. Mayor Bradley of Los Angeles and Mayor O'Connor of San Diego had been invited to co-chair the first working session—Urban Realities: Past and Present. Very early in his opening remarks, Mayor Bradley stated that the problems in cities are "reinforced within the pages and images of the news and entertainment media, which inflate the acknowledged problems of cities into gruesome headline-size stories. They give little space to what cities *have* done. They don't talk about access for business, values of diversity, contributions of libraries, museums, universities."[9] Then Mayor O'Connor added that perceptions in the press were one of the biggest problems the mayors face "because the press always reports the troubled parts." She said, "We must address how we'll package ourselves to the press, not just to D.C."

The mayors returned repeatedly to the "image problems" of cities, and to consideration of press strategies for dealing with them. Mayor Bradley was the first to suggest a strategy he and others have followed since the Summit. "You know as you run your campaigns it's *repetition* that finally gets the message across. We have to repeat these statements in different forums and in different conditions and by different people. I think that it is going to be up to us to organize and orchestrate that kind of repetition so that we change the image and get this message in all the places it needs to go."

Mayor Flynn argued most clearly for giving the journalists new angles. He held up a picture from that Sunday *New York Times* with the caption, "Mayors Call for More Federal Aid for the Cities," and asked theoretically, "You know where that's going to go, don't you? Nowhere." He continued, "I talked to a journalist yesterday, and he said, 'Isn't your message the same as it is every single place you go? You say the same thing in Chicago that you said in Washington, and you're saying it down here in New York. . . Why should I write about this?"

Mayor Rice of Seattle suggested a new angle: "I think that the best headline that we can possibly make Tuesday noon would be 'Mayors Develop a New Strategy for Better Education' because it would show vision, have public support, and it's a true long-term solution. . . . If we can talk people, especially children, and not cities, then we are getting there. . . . The public is willing to pay for certain things, not everything. They'll pay for children, not cities."

Mayor Abramson opined, "You know, one good story, one good half-hour show on the Bill Cosby show focused on a child coming home from school dealing with an issue of homelessness or AIDS or something urban-focused can carry a lot more of a message than any speech any one of us could give. . . ."

Mayor Scheibel said, "Let's talk a minute about the '92 elections. . . that might strike the media's fancy. . . . Maybe the mayors should say we are going to be looking at the candidates, . . . look[ing] at the issues and mak[ing] sure they raise the issues." Mayor Fraser agreed, and said a natural opportunity would be to tie it to the presidential candidate debates, suggesting that *mayors* question the candidates rather than journalists. Another mayor suggested groups of mayors go together to major cities, as SWAT teams, and lobby the press and interested citizens with their ideas and plans. Still another urged that the Summit mayors go together to see President Bush and the chairs of major congressional committees.

Several of the mayors had other ideas of what would capture media attention, and some had come to the Summit with prepared proposals. For example, Mayor Flynn offered a "Competitive Cities Act." Other mayors talked about innovative public/private partnerships, and still others urged elimination of boundaries between the cities and their surrounding suburbs.

As the day's sessions drew to a close, Mayor Flynn said, "I'd like to see us walk out of here with a unified strategy. . . saying these cities are strong, and we're going to propose a specific agenda, lobby behind it, and fight for it." Mayor Bradley agreed and urged, "If you call it national security issues, you are more likely to get a sexy headline out of it."

That evening, while the mayors met with the press and selected guests at a dinner held to better communicate the ideas that would be put forth at the next day's press conference, the mayors' aides worked on a statement for that press conference. By 7 a.m. they had delivered to each mayor's hotel room a draft copy of "The Urban Compact" (see page 7). It contained all the major points made by the mayors the day before, organized into a five-page document with goals, objectives, and action items. Its preamble declared that the social compact had frayed, and that American cities, therefore, must enter into new partnerships. The first section of the report focused on the kinds of new urban partnerships that could be developed, while the second discussed the role of cities in a global economy. The third and last section described fiscal challenges.

While a major goal of the document was to transform the views of journalists, only two of the objectives and action items specifically involved the media: "Identify and develop partnerships with all levels of government as well as with business, education, media and labor"[10] and "Meet with executives from major television networks and movie studios to seek inclusion of realistic and balanced urban themes in both television programming and movie production."[11]

Before the morning session began, several mayors clustered around copies of Milwaukee papers with stories headlined: "Mayors to Say Plight of Cities Is a National Security Concern" and "Mayors Seek to Boost the Image of Cities." Mayor Cooke commented, "I just hope that we can convince the press of New York and the rest of the national media to pick up on those two headlines."

Led by Mayors Rice and Cooke, the mayors made minor changes and approved section after section of the document. Then the mayors' attention turned to the press release and the format of the press conference. Several in the group thought the press release and Mayor Dinkins' prepared closing statement both exuded too much of the old, tin-cup feeling, and wanted them changed.

As the aides went off to do more rewriting, Mayor Dinkins described the press conference plan: Standing on a raised platform, at a podium, surrounded by the mayors, who were also to be standing, Dinkins would read his prepared statement. (Silverman said she had settled on this format because she thought it would provoke a sense of urgency.) And then the mayors would answer questions. Dinkins warned them that "The New York press is tough," predicting the press would ask about the costs of what the mayors proposed and about when they would meet with the president and congressional leaders. Dinkins suggested they all plan their answers carefully.

The closing press conference. The closing press conference proceeded as planned. As Dinkins spoke, the seventy to eighty journalists in attendance were reading copies of the press release and "In the National Interest." Much, but not all, of the tin-cup approach had been excised or moved. However, some of Dinkins's remarks reflected the old image, reminding the audience that former Mayor John Lindsay had taken New York's case to Washington, and it had resulted in the revenue-sharing program that had helped many cities in subsequent decades. Dinkins closed with the statement that the mayors had come together to "seek a new renaissance for the cities of the nation."

The first reporter to ask a question made it clear that the old image had not disappeared. "But Lindsay moved in a time of economic growth. This is a different time. Where would the money come from now for your plans?" Mayor Flynn responded, "Mayor Dinkins got us to focus on the strengths of our cities, and we're doing such things as filing a Competitive Cities Act. We didn't rehash what we need funded, but talked about self-help proposals. Some require changes in attitudes toward cities, as sources of culture and so on."

In this way, in response to questions from journalists, each and every mayor made a comment, often emphasizing points made during the preceding working sessions. They all made clear they supported the final document, and they denied significant conflict or disagreements among themselves. Several emphasized the political power they represented and how they could use their combined strength to force attention on the issues of cities in the 1992 elections.

AFTER THE SUMMIT

Most of the Summit mayors had left New York City by the time the next day's *New York Times*[12] appeared with a picture and story headlined, "Mayors Plead for More Federal Cooperation, and Money for Cities." The *Times* headline and article suggested that the mayors' media strategy was only partially successful, at least initially, in providing a new framework for conceptualizing the issues. Scattered television stories appearing immediately after the Summit focused on the needs of cities for more federal aid to deal with their problems, reflecting the old tin-cup image. However, several local television and print stories also mentioned the upbeat approaches and suggestions for solutions their hometown mayors had expressed at the Summit, and several included the "mighty engine" metaphor.

Throughout the rest of the fall, winter, and spring, many of the mayors continued to emphasize points made at the Summit, and these appeared in editorials, op-ed pieces, and other news stories. By the following June, one observer commented, "I would venture to say that there has been a decided turn in the [New York] *Times* to a sympathetic view of cities—in fact, not dissimilar to broad themes from the Summit."[13]

FURTHER OBSERVATIONS AND CONCLUSIONS

Because of the media's watchdog role in a democracy,[14] journalists tend to be suspicious of anything politicians say to them, especially in the context of a staged or pseudo event,[15] such as the closing Summit press conference. They expect politicians' comments and announcements to be self-serving. "In the National Interest" was prepared for and released *first* to the press, though copies were to accompany a request from Mayor Dinkins for a January meeting (subsequently postponed because of the war in the Persian Gulf) of all the Summit mayors with President Bush.

Although relatively short and readable, the document was long and complicated enough that it could not be digested quickly in the glare of floodlights and repartee of the press conference. Reporters may not have had time to read it carefully before they had to submit stories for afternoon papers or news shows, making it more likely they would rely on preexisting perceptions. The accompanying press release and statement by Mayor Dinkins were shorter, but, according to one journalist, seemed to contain somewhat mixed messages. Most of the journalists at the closing press conference were from New York media, and, while looking for new angles, they were clearly still influenced by prevailing negative views of urban problems. However, the reporters did seem to sense the mayors' unanimity, sense of urgency, and insistence that the old story was no longer the whole story.

In smaller, local markets (such as Milwaukee) where the mayors are more dominant and more often a major source of news, the journalists appear to have been more open to the new framing of urban issues being pushed by the Summit mayors and to have included more points from Summit documents. In all cities, the subsequent coverage and op-ed pieces indicate the mayors followed Mayor Bradley's admonition to *repeat* the new message in as many ways and places as possible.

It is, however, too soon to tell whether the repetition of the Summit message in the hometown and New York media will have the effect of building the agenda the mayors hoped for. The mayors' message is, after all, very complex. Moreover, the mayors chose to avoid conflict, an ingredient journalists' training and instincts teach them to look for, and one that has traditionally increased media attention to an issue. The mayors' unanimity—despite their different political ideologies and parties—was questioned by several disbelieving journalists who asked in many ways what the mayors had *disagreed* about.

The mighty engine metaphor may be attractive to business interests, but without compelling anecdotes, it may have seemed to the reporters unlikely to attract many viewers or readers. There was only one visual at the closing press conference—the mayors huddled together on a platform. While afternoon and early evening broadcasts reported the press conference, the *New York Times* headline seemed to set the tone for more analytic pieces.

With more time for reflection, perhaps the journalists could have been persuaded to view *their* best interests as getting the mayors' message across in their own locales and in Washington, D.C. If cities don't prosper, more businesses, including media businesses, will fail. It is likely media managers could be persuaded by the mayors' message about the long-term impacts of persistently negative images of cities—the fear, distrust, and anomie such images generate—especially when they are not counterbalanced by other positive images of innovation and problem solving.

Newspaper executives, hit hard by long-term declines in urban readership and the recent recession, have already begun thinking along these lines,[16] and many are making moves to be more positive in order to attract or win back readers, especially the young[17] and suburbanites.

But from the standpoint of city government, this approach has its own difficulties. For example, papers are printing more "soft," "useful" news on parenting, hobbies, health and fitness, community group activities, and other items of personal interest. Alarming to many, to make room for these "info-tainment" pieces the same papers are said to be "nuggetizing"[18] "hard" government and legislative news, doing fewer investigations, and covering city activities significantly less. One author refers to urban affairs (city hall and city government) as the "deserted" beat.[19] "Many editors concede that the routine government story has been a clear casualty of the move toward reader-friendly journalism," but there is a debate as to whether this represents a "return to a kind of community-based journalism that flourished years ago," or is a profit-driven failure of the media to live up to its obligation in a democratic society to provide news the people "need to give informed consent."[20]

Researchers also note the lessening of coverage of city government and urban problems and its costs: "With urban problems off the national agenda, mayors have a harder time convincing reporters (and voters) that city problems result, not just from actions of local officials, but also from nation-wide economic and social conditions."[21] One wonders if the editors' perceptions of declining interest of the public in government and city news are accurate, or whether the public is simply disinterested in the staged events that constitute so much of modern urban and government news. Clearly, the mayors' perception that they needed to change the lenses, and the frames of reference reporters use when writing about urban issues, was correct. It remains to be seen whether the "mighty engine" will turn out to have been the right vehicle for the job.

ENDNOTES

1. Number quoted by Mayor Dinkins in the opening press conference.

2. Phrase used by Mayor Dinkins in a speech (*New York Times*, September 13, 1990, p. 1) and subsequently adopted as a Summit theme.

3. And other politicians, as well.

4. A journalistic norm shared by journalists and their editors and producers is that for a news story to "have legs," to be continued beyond the first initial report, there must be new angles.

5. Many students of the media believe that most journalists are basically storytellers, and it excites them when news can also be turned into a "good" story—one that is interesting to write and to read or hear, develops and changes from day to day, and has important or interesting consequences. (See, for example, Gaye Tuchman, *Making News: A Study in the Construction of Reality* (New York: The Free Press, 1978).

6. Interviews with Sandra Silverman, during Summit and on March 6, 1991.

7. For example, A. Gordon, J. Heinz, S. Divorski, and M. Gordon, "Public Information and Public Access," *Northwestern Law Review*, vol. 68, no. 2 (May-June 1973): 280–308, discusses strategies for achieving positive and negative valences.

Dinkins's own press staff would concentrate on him, but the planners needed to provide for the other mayors, most of whom would not be bringing their local media with them.

8. Advance summaries of day's events.

9. Quotations of mayors during the working sessions are from transcriptions.

10. "In the National Interest," p. 3.

11. Ibid., p. 4.

12. November 13, 1991, p. 13.

13. Ronald Berkman, personal communication, June, 1991.

14. For example, see Robert Entman, *Democracy without Citizens* (New York: Oxford University Press, 1989).

15. Daniel Boorstin coined the term "pseudo event" to capture the idea that staged events are not news events in the traditional meaning of the phrase. The most common pseudo event, perhaps, is the press conference. Politicians and media strategists have learned which times of days, which days of the week, and which locations are most likely to draw journalists, and they have learned they need to say something newsworthy and unavailable elsewhere. They also try to get across preferred angles and emphases in press kits containing news releases, fact sheets, lists of other contacts, feature story ideas, and sometimes even sample legislation. (See Fay L.Cook, Tom R. Tyler, Edward Goetz, Margaret T. Gordon, David L. Protess, Donna M.Leff, and Harvey Molotch, "Media and Agenda Setting: Effects on the Public, Interest Group Leaders, Policy Makers and Policy," *Public Opinion Quarterly*, 47 (1983): 16–35. Other staged events can be much more elaborate: demonstrations, gala dinners, anniversary conferences, television, or parties. Sometimes they are designed especially for the visuals needed by TV, as described by Milwaukee Mayor Nordquist's press secretary, Steve McKay, who reported planning an event in which Nordquist joined sanitation crews as they cleaned up alleys in the central city. (See also Clarence Jones, *How to Speak TV, Print and Radio* (Tampa, FL: Video Consultants, 1991). Often the success of these events is evaluated in terms of the number of journalists who attend and the amount and nature of resulting press coverage.

16. Personal interview with Michael Fancher, editor, *Seattle Times*, March 12, 1991.

17. Only 24 percent of those under thirty-five years of age said in answer to a *Los Angeles Times* poll that they "read yesterday's paper," as opposed to 67 percent in 1965, according to Carl Sessions Stepp in "When Readers Design the News," *Washington Journalism Review* 3, no. 3 (April 1991): 20–24.

18. Melvin Mencher, quote in ibid, p. 24.

19. Cited in Reese Cleghorn, "The Deserted Beat," *Washington Journalism Reveiw*, 10, no. 3 (April 1988): 5.

20. See Stepp, "When Readers Design the News," p. 24.

21. Martin Linsky and Stephen Bates, "Big-City Mayors and the Press, 1966–86," forthcoming.

APPENDIX:

DEMOGRAPHIC AND ECONOMIC DATA, 1960–90

BY ROLAND ANGLIN, RUTGERS UNIVERSITY

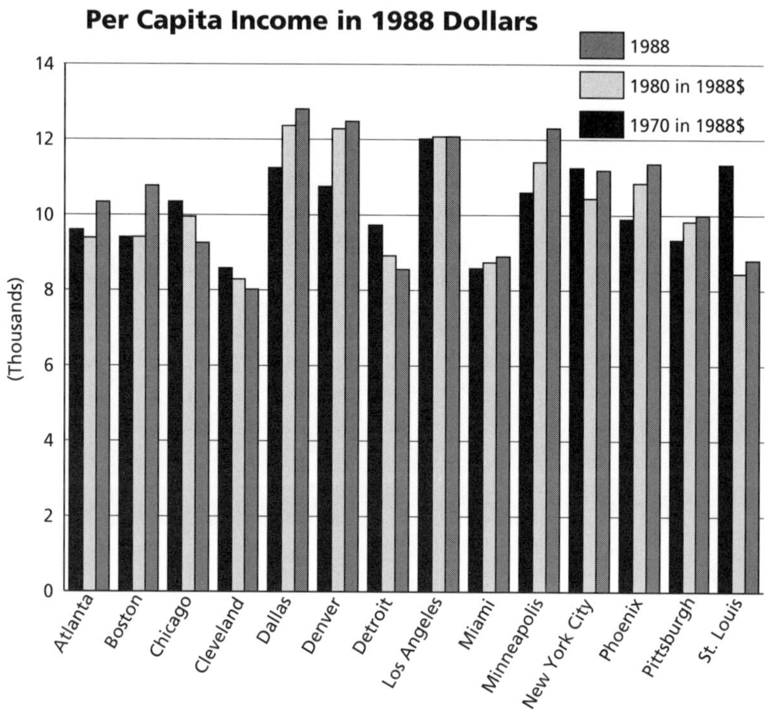

Income Per Capita (1988 Dollars)

	1970	1980	1988
Atlanta	9,602	9,391	10,341
Boston	9,411	9,414	10,774
Chicago	10,351	9,957	9,262
Cleveland	8,583	8,287	8,018
Dallas	11,248	12,368	12,816
Denver	10,752	12,286	12,490
Detroit	9,736	8,926	8,552
Los Angeles	12,021	12,075	12,081
Miami	8,583	8,738	8,904
Minneapolis	10,597	11,403	12,302
New York City	11,251	10,442	11,188
Phoenix	9,897	10,845	11,363
Pittsburgh	9,344	9,831	9,998
St. Louis	11,337	8,443	8,799

Source: *The County and City Data Fact Book* 1970–1988, Bureau of the Census

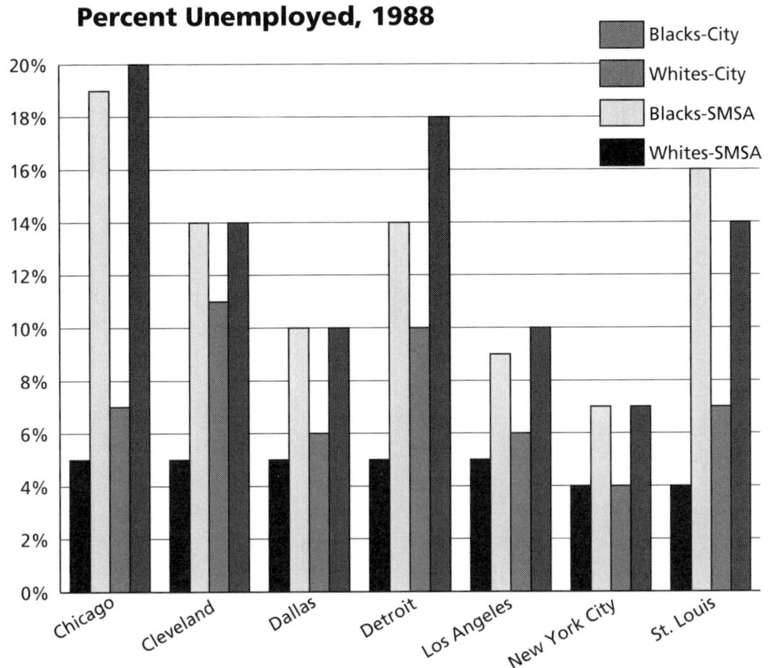

Percent Unemployed, 1988

	Whites-SMSA	Blacks-SMSA	Whites-City	Blacks-City
Chicago	5	19	7	20
Cleveland	5	14	11	14
Dallas	5	10	6	10
Detroit	5	14	10	18
Los Angeles	5	9	6	10
New York City	4	7	4	7
St. Louis	4	16	7	14

Source: *The County and City Data Fact Book* 1988, Bureau of the Census

Percent Below the Poverty Level

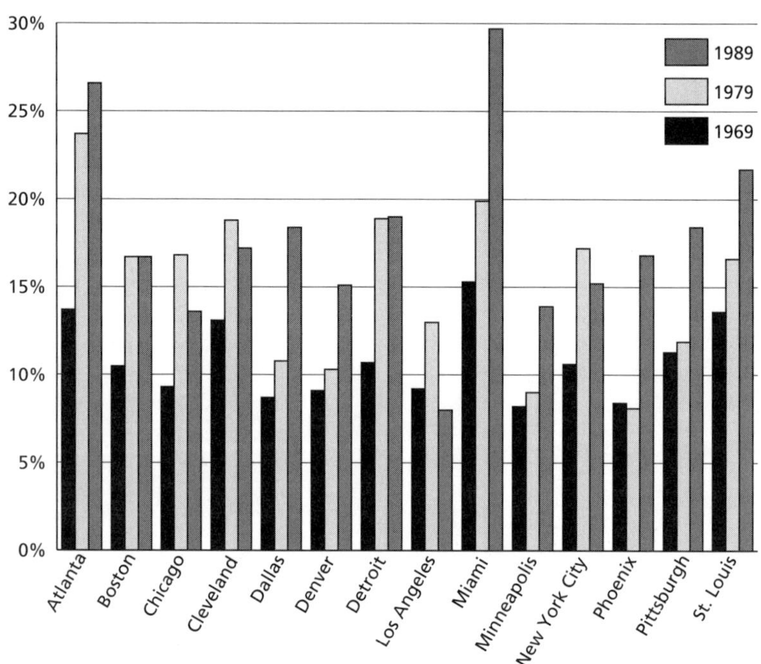

Percent Below Poverty Level

	1969	1979	1989
Atlanta	13.7	23.7	26.6
Boston	10.5	16.7	16.7
Chicago	9.3	16.8	13.6
Cleveland	13.1	18.8	17.2
Dallas	8.7	10.8	18.4
Denver	9.1	10.3	15.1
Detroit	10.7	18.9	19.0
Los Angeles	9.2	13.0	8.0
Miami	15.3	19.9	29.7
Minneapolis	8.2	9.0	13.9
New York City	10.6	17.2	15.2
Phoenix	8.4	8.1	16.8
Pittsburgh	11.3	11.9	18.4
St. Louis	13.6	16.6	21.7

Source: *The County and City Data Fact Book* 1969–1989, Bureau of the Census

Number of Manufacturing Establishments

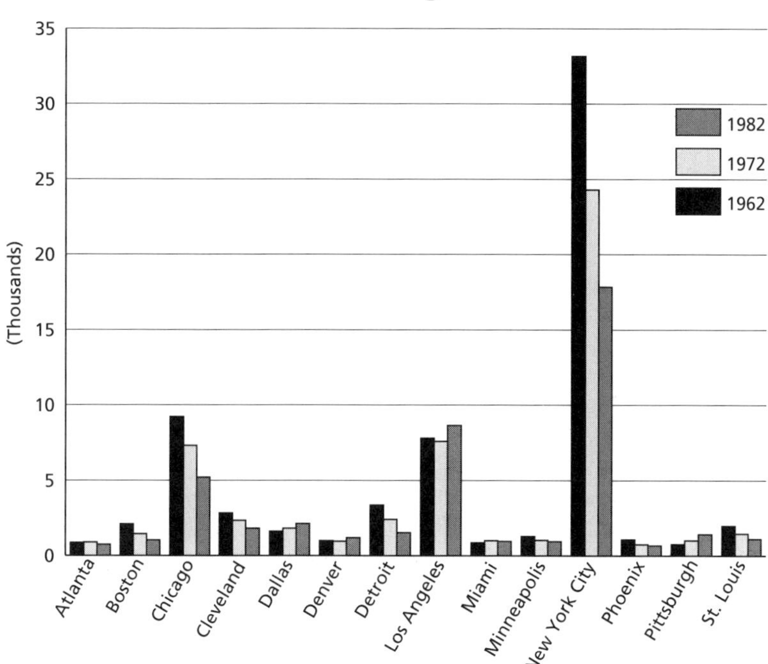

Number of Manufacturing Establishments

	1962	1972	1982
Atlanta	861	888	741
Boston	2,086	1,439	1,032
Chicago	9,221	7,310	5,203
Cleveland	2,821	2,336	1,812
Dallas	1,612	1,809	2,116
Denver	987	952	1,193
Detroit	3,370	2,398	1,518
Los Angeles	7,801	7,596	8,647
Miami	860	997	948
Minneapolis	1,283	1,026	938
New York City	33,179	24,306	17,848
Phoenix	1,073	749	671
Pittsburgh	763	1,004	1,417
St. Louis	1,970	1,461	1,107

Source: *The County and City Data Fact Book* 1962–1982, Bureau of the Census

Number of Retail Establishments

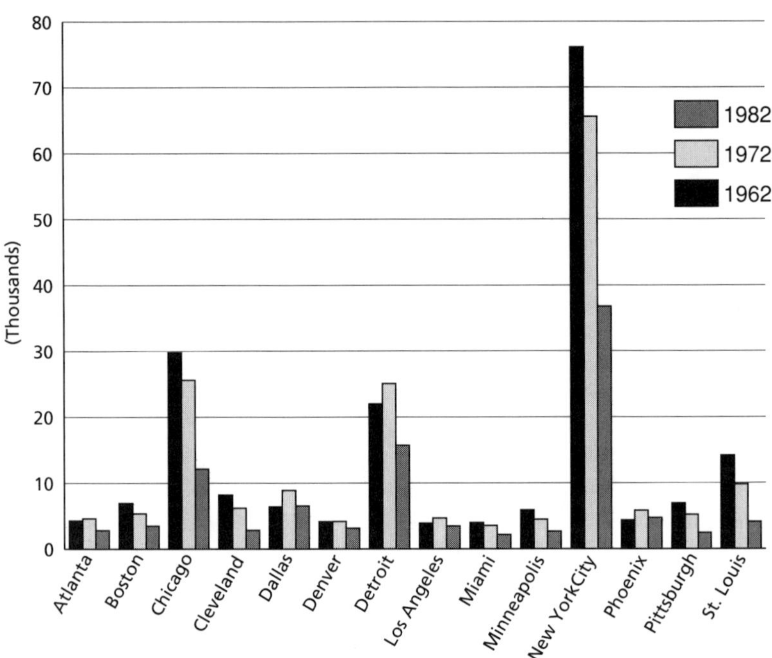

Number of Retail Establishments

	1962	1972	1982
Atlanta	4,276	4,603	2,804
Boston	6,940	5,363	3,467
Chicago	29,775	25,615	12,154
Cleveland	8,177	6,178	2,842
Dallas	6,394	8,882	6,513
Denver	4,131	4,159	3,132
Detroit	22,007	25,086	15,738
Los Angeles	3,894	4,659	3,458
Miami	3,974	3,529	2,141
Minneapolis	5,876	4,468	2,646
New York City	76,167	65,570	36,813
Phoenix	4,337	5,815	4,714
Pittsburgh	6,909	5,191	2,453
St. Louis	14,206	9,768	4,125

Source: *The County and City Data Fact Book* 1962–1982, Bureau of the Census

Number of Service Establishments

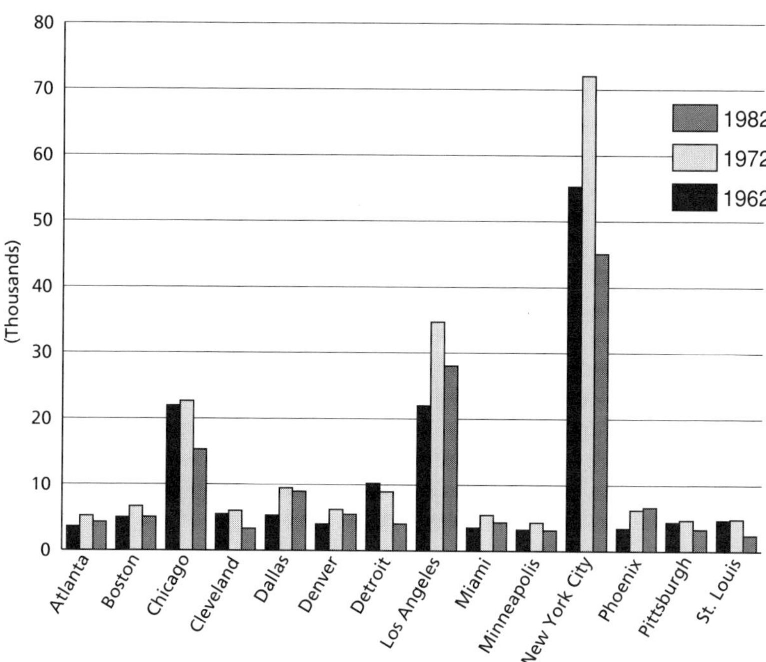

Number of Service Establishments

	1962	1972	1982
Atlanta	3,584	5,212	4,271
Boston	4,987	6,672	5,039
Chicago	21,957	22,648	15,312
Cleveland	5,500	6,022	3,326
Dallas	5,304	9,467	8,930
Denver	4,000	6,215	5,463
Detroit	10,233	8,907	4,058
Los Angeles	21,986	34,714	28,024
Miami	3,509	5,421	4,312
Minneapolis	3,217	4,276	3,137
New York City	55,320	72,051	45,087
Phoenix	3,437	6,204	6,589
Pittsburgh	4,368	4,686	3,286
St. Louis	4,674	4,821	2,397

Source: *The County and City Data Fact Book* 1962–1982, Bureau of the Census

ABOUT THE AUTHORS

Roland Anglin
Assistant Professor, Rutgers University, New Brunswick

Ronald Berkman
Professor and Acting Dean, City University of New York Office of
Urban Affairs

Joyce F. Brown
Vice Chancellor for Urban Affairs and Development, City University
of New York

David Collins
Research Associate, University of Louisville

Lena Lundgren Gaveras
Research Associate, University of Chicago

Arthur S. Goldberg
Research Director, Robert F. Wagner Sr. Institute, Graduate Center,
City University of New York

Margaret T. Gordon
Dean, School of Public Affairs, University of Washington, Seattle

Richard Nathan
Provost, Rockefeller College, State University of New York, Albany

Frances Fox Piven
Professor, City University of New York Graduate Center

Daniel Sanders
Research Associate, University of Louisville

H. V. Savitch
Professor, College of Urban Affairs, University of Louisville

William Julius Wilson
Distinguished Professor, Department of Sociology, University of Chicago